SURVIVAL PLUS

Using Realistic Management Techniques to Conquer Internal and External Threats to Company Success

SURVIVAL PLUS

A MANAGEMENT HANDBOOK

Martin Weiss

CHILTON BOOK COMPANY RADNOR PENNSYLVANIA

Published in Radnor, Pennsylvania 19089, by Chilton Book Company

Designed by William E. Lickfield
Manufactured in the United States of America

Library of Congress Cataloging in Publication Data

Weiss, Martin
Survival plus: a management handbook using realistic management techniques to conquer internal and external threats to company success/ Martin Weiss.
p. cm.
Includes bibliographical references.
ISBN 0-8019-7983-8
1. Industrial management—Handbooks, manuals, etc. I. Title.
HD31.W446 1989 89–42858
658—dc20 CIP

1 2 3 4 5 6 7 8 9 0 8 7 6 5 4 3 2 1 0 9

To PETIE
who gave me love and encouragement
and
To OLIVER
who kept me company

Contents

Introduction

THE odds of being successful in business are stacked against you. If your company makes it through the difficult and treacherous early years, the chances of remaining a viable, independent business for a reasonable length of time improve—but are still not a sure thing. The battle for business survival is continuous; even business entities in the billion-dollar class find themselves fighting for their lives. In recent years, scores of once highly profitable corporations engaged in the oil drilling industry found themselves in or near bankruptcy; several major airlines teeter on the brink of ruin; household names in manufacturing have been out-priced, out-engineered, out-manufactured, and put out of business. Regardless of the industry, service, or product, business managers and owners are in a constant struggle for survival.

The Darwinian theory of "survival of the fittest" is an oversimplification when it comes to business. To start with, how would you define "fittest" in a business sense? Financial strength? Excellent product reputation and recognition? State-of-the-art technology? A dedicated and loyal work force? Good management? Hard work? Each of these factors and others, plus some elements of luck, are involved in the highly competitive business world. A business, its management, and the scope of problems encountered evolves over time; so too must its skills.

The struggle for continued business survival in a highly competitive, hostile, and dangerous environment is the name of the game. I advocate "looking out for #1"—yourself and your company. If you are skilled at stretching your cash, clever in anticipating and avoiding problems, or adept in problem or crisis management, the better the chances for survival. When your business survives, those who depend upon you—family, employees, customers, suppliers, creditors—are also better off.

There has been a growing social phenomenon in recent years—open disparagement of earning a profit, as if that were some crime or sordid motive for which the businessperson should feel guilty. Business's public relations response to an increasingly hostile (to business) public environment has been an attempt, usually by the larger companies, to obscure their profit-making objective with a patina of positive social contributions. That many businesses have been guilty of a callous despoiling of the environment, exploitation of employees, production of shoddy and defective products, bribes and conspiracies, all in the search for profits, is true and undeniable. Nevertheless, that does not make the profit objective itself any less honorable or important. The vast majority of companies earn their profits by hard work, smart management, innovation, and risk-taking.

There is no one formula for success; no guaranteed-to-work strategic planning process. Business success does not always come to those most deserving or most qualified. There is always at least one competitor who is seeking out your customers, your market niche, your future. Do you always have to employ "cutthroat" tactics to survive or win? Only you can be the judge of that. One thing is certain: nice guys can and often do finish last.

Some of the ideas and comments included in this book may disturb you if you are an advocate of "playing it by the book." You may consider a few of the suggestions and remarks to be inappropriate at best or illegal at worst. Pick and choose what you feel is useful and what you are most comfortable with. Let your own conscience or survival needs be your guide.

Some standard management concepts and methods are mentioned only briefly, without extensive explanation. If they are unfamiliar to you, please look into them in greater detail. While you may feel that the problems and issues you face are unique, it is certain that someone else faced a similar situation and managed to emerge victorious.

The names of the companies and their executives used as representative examples in this book are fictional, but the situations, responses, and actions described are real and true to life.

Without meaning to give offense to the many thousands of successful and competent women engaged in owning and/or managing businesses, I will use the masculine gender in a generic sense to refer to both men and women.

PART 1

Forewarned is Forearmed

WE may be doomed to repeat the mistakes of history unless we learn from them, and the same may be said for the world of business. There are no new problems in business, just the same ones that occur, with minor variations, over and over again. The multinational conglomerate may have a big balance sheet, tens of thousands of employees, and a famous brand name, but it still will have to deal with the same types of problems and challenges as those faced by the president of a small local company producing custom-made truck bodies.

Some problems can be avoided by management foresight. Others will be unavoidable even with an enlightened management team. Either way, every businessman or woman can learn something from the experiences of others.

Chapter 1

Dangers Ahead

What Hit Us?

Optimism, confidence, and foresight are vital ingredients that must be present when you are in business. True, there are times when events may shake everyone up, but that's precisely when you will need a clear head in order to make an honest reappraisal of the situation. All too often a management group seems surprised and shocked to suddenly discover their company is in serious trouble. Almost always, if management had been doing its job properly, that situation could and should have been anticipated and dealt with before it reached a critical and dangerous level. Management, however, allowed optimism to be replaced by wishful thinking. Its confidence became an ego trip, and, instead of exercising foresight, management became a victim of its own tunnel vision. The result: a company in a crisis, confronted with possible bankruptcy and ruin.

Surprise, Surprise!

Many of the situations that can bring a company to its knees are caused by external factors, such as changes in its market, changes in technology, or cyclical gyrations in the financial community. While a company has no direct control over such events, it can try to anticipate such problems by staying in touch with what's going on in the world.

A key task for any company is to keep its collective eyes open and remain sensitive to all the forces that can exert influence, both negative and positive, and shape tomorrow's reality. Every company should monitor changes in trends, fashions, and fads and be alert to warning signs appearing in other industries. In addition, it should watch what is happening with its customers and competitors. If technology is important, the company must remain constantly vigilant for the first sign of new methods, developments, directions, or concepts that can have an impact on its own products, processes, or methods.

Because, today, all businesses exist in a global environment and are subject to myriad forces and influences coming from every direction, having a parochial viewpoint is dangerous. Where should the company be looking? Everywhere. Who should be looking? Everyone—and with a sensitivity that will override any individual's preconceived notions or fixed beliefs. "But I thought . . ." is a belated and plaintive response from a short-sighted executive or manager.

A company should be prepared to use outside consultants and advisers as sources for input and observations. Frequently, an executive group becomes so engrossed in the minutiae of the daily activities of business that it is unable to see what may be obvious to an independent outsider. Executives, being normal human beings, sometimes suffer from personal blind spots and prejudices that can spell disaster for a company's future. Somewhere along the way they have closed their minds, refusing to listen to suggestions or advice or learn from the experiences of others.

Every executive should take the time to read and review material from a variety of sources, not just the usual industry trade papers. With so many excellent publications dealing with a wide variety of business and general subjects, some progressive companies maintain their own in-house "free library," which contains an extensive, perhaps eclectic collection of books on economics, management, entrepreneurship, world history and events, and books written by well-known business leaders that an executive may not ordinarily buy for himself. Subscriptions are kept up to date for many business and current-events magazines. Maintained in files accessible to practically all employees on a sign-out basis, the company library is an excellent way for executives and employees to increase their knowledge, scope, and awareness of business and the real world. While using the library is purely voluntary, top management can set an example for the rest of the company by using the library regularly.

In addition, time should be set aside periodically for freeform conferences among executive and supervisory groups on a broad range of topics that now or in the future may effect company operations. An exchange of ideas among this group may lead to new directions and horizons for the company and help break down existing barriers and antagonisms created during the stress of normal business operations. Ideally, these meetings should be held outside the office or factory.

Rough Spots and Pitfalls

When a company gets into trouble, the underlying cause (in addition to management's failure to do its job in the first place) is probably one or more of the situations outlined below. Several situations can exist at the same time, although, like anyone who is ill, a company under duress may fall victim to a variety of ills quickly. In the true-life example outlined below, the management of Colorful Products Company made a number of errors in judgment that ultimately brought a profitable, long-established company to its knees.

For twenty years, Colorful Products Company had designed and manufactured precision machinery used by a segment of the commercial printing industry. The company had a well-deserved reputation for producing high-quality products. Though the family-owned company was thinly capitalized, operations had usually been profitable, although some years were significantly better than others. Sales had reached $20 million a year, with most of the revenue derived from products that were customizations of basic in-house designs adapted to meet a customer's specific requirements. Accordingly, practically all manufacturing and assembly activities were geared to a "short-run/make-to-order/rapid turnover" concept, with the scheduling, procurement, and production tied into each customer's order. Other than some basic materials common to all of its products (sheet metal, bar stock, hardware), most of the company's inventory investment at any one time was usually in work-in-process for specific customer orders. In general, most orders were completed within ninety days, so the limited capital base was rarely strained.

In the company's twenty-first year, engineers developed product "X," which was introduced and demonstrated at a printing industry trade show. Product "X," though complex and costly, with a selling price five times higher than the company's other products, appeared to be what the industry needed. Colorful Products was looking forward to increasing its sales volume by five to seven million dollars a year. The company was flooded with orders and customer down-payments.

The company immediately went into production, placing large purchase orders for materials, parts, and components and hiring additional employees. The company continued to produce its traditional products as well.

After two decades of slow but steady growth, the company's future seemed secure and rosy. Unfortunately, its thin capital structure proved insufficient to support the increased demand for working capital, further aggravated by the inevitable "glitches" in production common to new-product manufacturing. The company learned that the manufacturing cycle for product "X" was not ninety days, as with its other products, but six months. Even without any engineering problems or the need to train new employees, the company's usual short-run, quick turnover, job-order manufacturing process was inappropriate for product "X." More and more money was needed for raw materials and work-in-process for increasingly longer periods of time. In desperation, the company, which had never been a borrower before, turned to its local bank. The bank officials, having known and respected the company and its management for twenty years, and upon seeing the tremendous influx of orders for product "X," quickly agreed to provide a credit line for $6 million of demand debt (at several "points" over the floating prime rate). The bank also took a lien on all the company's assets.

Drawing down on the funds now available, the company struggled to manufacture its new design while simultaneously attempting to work out the "bugs" now showing up on the manufacturing floor and at some customers who had received early shipments. Just as the company was resolving these problems, its marketing management chose to announce and demonstrate a new, more advanced model, product "Y," with even more desirable features. Almost immediately, many customers switched their orders from product "X" to product "Y," leaving the company with enormous amounts of inventory components for product "X."

In fact, the company was totally unprepared—financially or technically—to produce product "Y," yet it tried to adjust its already overburdened manufacturing operations and strained financial position to produce another new, not yet debugged, prototype.

The manufacturing problems, delays, and interest costs generated big losses while the bank debt continued to increase. Over the next two years, the company drew down $5 million from its line of credit but still had not solved all its problems. The bank canceled the remaining $1 million of credit. Using the threat of calling the demand debt (secured by the Colorful Products Company assets), the bank forced the company into a supervised "workout" situation.

While the bank did not put the company out of business (it would have gotten only 10 percent to 25 percent on the dollar), it did force the liquidation of certain assets (including patents), reducing inventory, and laying off key engineering, manufacturing, and management personnel. All cash received was controlled by the bank (applied against the debt and interest), with a portion released to cover ongoing payroll and some vendors' invoices. The retrenchment reduced the company's sales volume to $10 million.

For all practical purposes, the company was now being run by the bank. Until the bank debt and accumulated interest was repaid, most corporate decisions would be made jointly by the company owners and the bank's representatives, with the bank having veto power. The company's future was on hold. In addition, if and when the company repaid the debt, it would need a massive infusion of new capital to remain a viable business, able again to look toward the future.

*

In retrospect, it is easy to see what mistakes the Colorful Products Company made, but in the euphoria of apparent success, matters do not always seem that clear and obvious.

In fact, the modes of business failure for young and seasoned companies alike usually fall into one of six categories: inadequate financial strength, failing to keep up in the marketplace, having out-of-date technology, poor management and a lack of leadership, systems failures, and internal strife.

Inadequate Financial Strength

Every business requires a certain minimum level of permanent capital to function—the working capital tied up in receivables and inventory; funds to provide the required equipment and facilities; cash flow to make debt and interest payments; and a reserve to be able to weather the inevitable up-and-down cycles. Conditions may change, however, and the company may soon find itself without adequate finances for its new circumstances.

For example, to respond to a competitor's initiative, a new-product development and manufacturing program becomes necessary, but the company is unable to fund it. As a result, it loses market share and its primary source of revenue. Perhaps an extension or stretch out in the normal "turnover-time" cycle of the business (buy/build inventory→sell/deliver→collect) occurs and the company cannot adjust to it financially.

Many companies fail or are placed in great jeopardy when they attempt to grow beyond their level of financial capacity. It isn't uncommon to see a company introduce a new product that generates more orders than it is able to handle. Management ramps up production, stretching out its accounts payable in the process. It borrows additional funds on a short-term basis and then finds its house-of-cards collapsing when there is a glitch (even a small one) in the product, in manufacturing, or in the market. Lenders and suppliers pressure management for immediate payment, forcing the company to divert its dwindling cash flow from supporting current operations to buy more time from the creditors, all the while hoping for some miracle. Management is no longer in control of the company's destiny. Instead, it is beholden to the bankers and creditors, who are trying to siphon as much as possible as quickly as possible without regard for the company's future.

The cost of borrowed funds, especially those with variable-rate interest, can reach a level beyond the earning and cash-generating capacity of the company. This creates a hemorrhage, a slow form of death, with the company keeping one nervous eye on the prime rate and the other on its shrinking asset base.

Obviously, losing money on a regular basis can erode financial resources to a level below what is needed for effective operations. Some companies in highly volatile industries seem to have a pattern of generating moderate to good earnings for a few years. Then they have a disaster year that wipes out a substantial portion of their accumulated equity. If the company stays in business long enough, the constant impairment of their resources keeps the company at marginal levels and impairs its ability to obtain additional financing.

The "mix" of the capital sources a company uses is also important. Relying too heavily on short-term debt is dangerous, especially when that debt is used to support a more or less permanent growth in sales. Leverage may be an excellent way to improve the return on shareholders' equity, but it also has its share of hazards. Sometimes management becomes overly confident regarding debt and capital, maintaining an attitude of "we can always get it when we need it." Sources of capital should never be taken for granted. Many successful, profitable companies have found themselves *persona non grata* when they have approached financial institutions on Wall Street or Main Street for reasons having nothing to do with the company itself.

Each of these situations and many others can convert a financially healthy company into a basket case in a surprisingly short time. Financial health is a fragile and variable condition that cannot be taken for granted by management, regardless of the company's size.

Failing in the Marketplace

The methods and requirements for reaching and appealing to existing and potential customers are constantly changing. A company's products, sales, and distribution system must stay current. Not all companies see the need for change or make a needed change. It isn't always a competitor that defeats you in the marketplace. Sometimes you do it to yourself. No market remains constant, and a management group that denies this fact will not succeed.

When a company derives a major portion of its sales revenue from one customer, that company and its future are exceptionally vulnerable. No matter how friendly and cooperative the relationship has been in the past, it is always possible to lose that customer, or be forced to give so many concessions (price, warranty, credit terms) that the health of the business suffers. Putting all or most of the company's eggs in one basket is a classic invitation to disaster.

Out-of-Date Technology

Over the last twenty-five years, thousands of companies, large and small, fell by the wayside because they failed to keep up with changes in technology. In fact, the pace of technological change is accelerating. It is difficult to imagine any company—whether manufacturing, service, or retail—not being affected in some way by technology. Changes in technology not only affect final product design and performance but also the internal processes used for engineering, research, manufacturing, assembly, quality control, distribution, marketing, and management. Lagging behind in technology and losing the competitive edge is another self-inflicted company killer.

The Human Factor

Not only can companies outgrow their facilities or their finances, but often they outgrow their own management as well. The talents and skills that were sufficient when the company's operations were smaller and less complex may now be totally inadequate. Personnel who have been with the company since the "old days" may have, over the years, received titles and promotions, rising to critical positions of responsibility for which they do not have the necessary vision or competence. The same can be said of some owner/founders who, even if still competent in relation to the company's larger size, are unwilling to delegate responsibility. They choose to retain and exercise a level of personal control that suffocates the management team and the company's future. Such situations are emotionally charged and difficult for a company to acknowledge, much less deal with. They are, nevertheless, high on the list of primary causes of business crisis or failure.

Sometimes top management has difficulty making the tough decisions, whether bringing in a new manufacturing executive over good, old, loyal Joe, who has been the factory manager for fifteen years; slashing expenses and getting "lean and mean" when profits slip; or canceling the endless research project that seems to have been swallowing up resources forever. Every time management fails to take necessary but tough action in critical areas, it weakens the company further.

Systems Failure

The absence of effective internal safeguards, checks and balances, routine followup, or audit trails are an invitation to disasters ranging from innocent blunders to outright fraud or theft. Sometimes the control systems are adequate but aren't followed consistently or are selectively ignored when they prove inconvenient. This pitfall is insidious because many of the resulting problems remain hidden until suddenly they burst on the scene with devastating effect. For example, shipments continue to be made to a customer whose account balance is large and considerably past due because the internal administrative system does not require approval by the credit department before an order is accepted and the shipment is made. Another example: A product development project is rushed to completion by the engineering department and released to production on the strength of one or two "working prototypes" without on-site field testing, quality assurance review, or revalidation of the anticipated manufacturing cost/selling price relationship. Another example: Consider the dangers to a company that has no formal, written "employee handbook" to guide supervisors and employees regarding the "who, what, how, and when" of company personnel policies and practices.

Not all dangers stem from loose controls. At times an internal system can be too tight and rigid, causing paralysis when quick response is needed, or stifling initiative and creativity.

It is not always easy to self-diagnose a company's systems' ills. Some show up only when they explode in your face; others remain hidden, continuing to erode company profitability and progress. Often it may take an outsider or newcomer to point out the problems in the system.

A Battle Royal from Within

A partnership or a company with a board of directors independent in whole or in part from top management may find itself engaged in a form of regicide—partner against partner, top management against the board, one clique of the board against another. In any case, the true victim will be the company, and the conflict will ultimately reach every employee. Whether the root cause is a conflict of direction for the company, a clash of personalities, a difference in style, or petty jealousy, if allowed to continue without resolution, the company will be seriously, perhaps fatally, wounded. Because the partners, board, or president cannot look downward in the organization for help in solving problems, they should seek qualified outside assistance as soon as possible.

Sometimes the conflict takes place at the next lower peer level, among the vice-presidents and other senior executives. Even then the effects will be the same. When dealing with that problem, the president and the board must be sure they understand the nature of the conflict and have all the pertinent facts before they make a move to resolve the conflict.

It Can Happen Here

Staying on top of the business situation demands the concerted, coordinated effort of many people. No business is invulnerable, not even yours. On a personal level, no manager is infallible, not even *you*. Learning some of the pitfalls that have sunk other businesses may help you keep yours healthy.

Chapter 2

Business Phases

AT some point, every business began as someone's dream—a germ of an idea that became reality because someone had the entrepreneurial spirit and drive to take the necessary steps and risks. There is not too much difference between "business venture" and "business adventure," for anyone starting a business is embarking on a quest filled with dangers, disappointments, exciting times, frustration, and hard work. Unfortunately, the frequency of failure by business start-ups is high, and individual effort is no guarantee of success. Once beyond the start-up phase, the businessperson is still fighting for survival against a formidable array of adversaries and obstacles. Those can include a competitor opening up just a few blocks away, a new technology coming out of Japan, a chronic shortage of capital, or the conflict between the demand for your time by your family and by your business. The list is endless and variable, as is the struggle.

The choices you as owner/manager must make to overcome the obstacles are influenced by the life phase of your company. Recognizing and understanding those phases will help prepare you to make the right decisions and set the right priorities.

There are seven major phases in the life of a company. Not all companies reach or successfully pass through every phase. Within each phase are personal and management options that lead to alternative futures for the company and you.

Phase 1: Genesis

Before one dollar is invested or one customer contacted, someone first must recognize the commercial possibilities in any venture. We have all encountered them, but few of us have recognized them until too late, and even fewer did something about them. What would most people have done in the following examples?

> Watching TV at home one evening, you're nibbling on some microwave popcorn, wishing it were tastier. Suddenly you get an idea: Why not flavor it with garlic, or cayenne pepper, or Italian herbs? You try it, it's good. Your family tries it. They like it, and so do many of your friends and neighbors. Someone, maybe your own inner voice, says, "Why don't you make and sell this stuff? It's a great idea. People will buy it by the bagful."
>
> Knowing that you're a capable and experienced computer programmer, your older brother, a dentist, asks for your help in setting up a system to track his appointments, maintain patient records, do the third-party insurance billing, and generally handle record-keeping and accounting for his practice. After several weeks' work, you develop a unique, comprehensive system that's easy to learn, simple to operate, and provides the framework to handle practically any medical practice. "I know fifty guys in our local dental association that desperately need something like this," your brother says to you. "Why don't I talk to them?"
>
> A close friend and neighbor of yours, a hobbyist and tinkerer, demonstrates a small battery-operated electronic module he made in his basement. When hung near his garden, the module silently but infallibly attracts and destroys only Japanese beetles. After telling you he designed and built it from scratch at a total cost of only $2.89, he asks you if you know of anyone interested in selling similar modules.

In each case, there seems to be the potential for a new business venture—an opportunity staring you in the face, waiting to be picked up, studied, investigated, perhaps even carried forward to the next phase. More of these "genesis" opportunities cross your path than you may realize, but most of us aren't observant, or we fail to convert our dreams into an action plan. Thus, the "genesis" phase of a business is actually a combination of three factors:

1. One or more individuals with the mind-set, emotional preparedness, and desire to become an entrepreneur, plus
2. A business idea or opportunity that is found or accidentally encountered, plus
3. Action—grasping the idea or opportunity and doing something positive about it.

Unless all three elements are present, little, if anything, will happen and only wishful thinking will prevail. However, under the right circumstances, the business moves into the next phase—start-up.

Phase 2: Start-up

The pro's and con's of the business idea have been weighed, the capital has been scraped together, leases are signed, equipment and inventory are purchased, maybe a few people are hired. Then, with a considerable amount of excitement and some natural trepidation, the business opens. Almost immediately your life changes. The fears and concerns you had earlier become real worries: Will enough customers and orders come in today? Will I have the right things in inventory? Will the cash last? You seem to be needed everywhere at once, and the pressure never stops. Every problem comes to you and every decision is made by you. You are totally immersed in the business, and every day is a struggle to survive to the next. Survival becomes an even more important objective than profit. You have three possibilities: giving up by selling out or closing up, succeeding so that you move to the next phase, or continuing to make the effort until the business either fails or moves into the next phase.

Phase 3: Touch and Go

The confusion of the "start-up" phase is now over. Things have sorted themselves out. Routines have been established and additional knowledge has been gained regarding the market, customers, inventory, and pricing. Still totally immersed in the business, you are trying to hire and train employees that can help you and take some of the load off. The business remains completely vulnerable to practically everything. You have stretched your capital as far as it can go, perhaps too far. It is still too early to say if the business will make it.

This phase, which can linger for a considerable length of time, may be the most difficult and aggravating so far. Things can go either way. While you may be tempted to chuck it all and move on to something else, the personal investment and commitments you made have you locked in. The business is practically worthless if sold, so you must either quit, taking the financial and emotional beating, or persevere until you reach the next phase.

Phase 4: Sustaining

A business reaching the "sustaining" stage is doing well enough to meet its bills with a little extra left over for you to take home. Customers are being serviced and a standard routine has been established. There is no longer a crisis every day. But, while the business does not take all your time, it still dominates your life. You still make all the decisions, delegating a minimum of responsibility and authority to other employees. You have standing orders and instructions that everyone follows, but things are generally done on an informal basis. You have little financial information available to assist you; your records are not much more than a checkbook and a few sales and inventory records. Perhaps an accountant comes in a few times a year to prepare the necessary tax forms and reports. Given its fragile organizational and financial strength, and its overall vulnerability, the business remains in a struggle for survival. It can continue like this for years, and many, perhaps most, small businesses do. Once having reached this stage, there are three possible alternatives: an increased effort to generate profits and move the company beyond the "sustaining" stage, remaining with the status quo, or failure. Choosing to make the effort to generate increased profits means renewing your personal commitment, and this means increased stress and an investment of more of your time—similar to the conditions that existed during the "start-up" phase. Risks will increase, and you will need to learn new skills and how to build an organization.

Phase 5: Attainment

You have now arrived. The company, though small, has developed into a profitable and stable enterprise with a reasonably assured future having only the normal (but still dangerous) business risks to which a small business is subject. You have time to spend with your family and for other pursuits. The company has competent personnel at the management level, as well as adequate policies, procedures, and systems for the current scope of operations. Finances are in good shape, as is the product and/or marketing position. Once again you are faced with several paths, each leading to a different phase: coasting along with the status quo, making an intense push for growth, or selling out.

With the company's stability more or less assured, (although there is always the potential for a major disruption from a number of external variables), you still devote time and attention to the business but take no major risks. Your competent staff allows you to spend less time at the office, and it no longer dominates your life. So long as nothing shakes its stability, the business can continue for years.

Another path available at any time is to sell out—to convert your equity and business value into cash. Selecting this path may enable you to move your life in totally new directions.

A third alternative is to make a concerted effort for growth—to push ahead in an attempt to become a bigger operation. There is a marked difference between this approach and accepting the status quo. While some nominal growth may come naturally to the company, perhaps almost effortlessly while in the status quo mode, the atmosphere is much less intense than when in a push for growth. For one thing, the company seeking growth usually must put a substantial portion of its financial integrity and stability at risk. The quest for growth will probably require developing new products and/or markets; finding new locations for stores, sales offices, or factories; increasing the investment in inventory and equipment; and hiring more employees. In short, the company is entering a phase not too dissimilar from the "start-up" phase.

Almost certainly, you will have to devote more time to the business. While the functions you will perform will be somewhat different than the "do-everything yourself" mode of the "start-up" phase, they will require special management talents. You will have to develop strategic and tactical plans and review and monitor those plans. Your ability to operate in an environment where you must delegate authority for activities and decision-making with so much at risk will be tested. You will be more vulnerable than ever to any lack of competence from the executives you have chosen, the systems and procedures under which the company operates, and the feedback you obtain from the management information system. Choosing the "push for growth" path, and with it the new, higher level of risk involved, raises the specter of bankruptcy, or being left to pick up the pieces in case of failure.

Phase 6: Growth

The business is growing steadily and significantly in sales and profits; in fact, it's almost like riding a runaway horse. The growth is consuming—no, demanding—more and more resources: capital, personnel, organization. Now you are faced with another problem: How do you manage such a beast? Does your success mean you can never back off? Is your executive team capable of handling these latest demands? Perhaps more important, are you?

In the growth phase, it is not unusual to find that a company has outgrown the abilities of the owner/manager. In fact, the growth phase produces considerable conflict within an organization. Executives with more drive and ambition than you may be pushing for objectives far beyond the scope you intended. If yours is a technology company, the complexity of the technologies may be increasing far beyond your level of understanding and knowledge.

The growth stage will require ongoing capital input, perhaps increasing debt, or offering a portion of the company's stock to the public to provide the resources needed to retain the momentum. You may be uncomfortable with either choice.

Once again, you have several alternative paths: turn the company over to professional managers, learn how to manage a company in this stage, pull back and stabilize operations at a less demanding stage, or sell out.

Sometimes an owner/manager will turn the reins of day-to-day leadership over to another manager, choosing instead to function as a member or chairman of the board, concentrating only on broad direction and policy matters. The company can then continue in its growth mode for as long as possible.

You can also choose to learn new management skills and develop your capacity to lead and be comfortable with the type of company you now have. While still a major force in day-to-day operations, you will have to grant more freedom and autonomy to your executive team. You must learn when and how to step away and not interfere with the other executives' operations. At all times, you must be alert to the possibility that you may become a victim of rising to a level beyond your own competence.

Sometimes, rather than aggressively pursuing the company's growth potential, an owner/manager may decide to take the company a step or two backwards. Certain opportunities are relinquished, but so are certain risks. The owner/manager adjusts operations to a comfort level that suits his or her lifestyle and needs. There are risks associated with this posture as well. The executive team may be more ambitious than the owner/manager and choose to leave, or trying to maintain the status quo actually results in the company falling behind and losing everything.

It is also possible to sell the company at this stage, and many companies are. With a good history of profitable growth and the potential for even more, the company can usually command a favorable price.

Phase 7: Maturity

Similar to the "attainment" phase, but at an entirely different level, a company reaches maturity when it has achieved a relatively assured and stable future. Profits are steady and significant. Capital resources are more than adequate to weather all but the most severe economic ill-winds. The period of rapid growth is over, and many of the internal problems associated with that period have evaporated. Much of the management effort is devoted to fine-tuning systems, methods, and overall company efficiency. "Steady as she goes" is the daily routine. Although the company could begin to stagnate and perhaps be caught with its pants down by some more aggressive competitor, an alert professional management should be able to avoid that possibility. Unfortunately, many companies, large and small (automobile, steel, and TV manufacturing in the United States, for example), fall victim to their own complacency, overconfidence, and loss of entrepreneurial zeal.

The Challenge of Ownership

Each of the seven business phases presents a different set of challenges. The question of whether you can successfully cope with the varied demands of those situations is vital. Even though the business itself is or can be a viable one, if you are unable or unwilling to make the necessary sacrifices for the demands on your time, lifestyle, emotions, and family, the business will fail to progress and prosper.

Chapter 3

Hazardous Times

SOMETIMES it seems as if your business lurches from one big internal problem to another. No matter how much you plan or try to anticipate the future, another crisis pops up and disrupts the organization and its timetable. The truth is, many of these internal crises are predictable but, given human nature, probably unavoidable. Nevertheless, it is wise to know what the crises are and be able to recognize their symptoms. By doing so, you may be able to put your finger on the problem early and take corrective actions.

In the Beginning

At the early stages of a company's existence, survival is usually entirely dependent upon the talent, knowledge, leadership, and extraordinary efforts of one person. Even in a partnership, one of the partners is usually more creative and vigorous. The ability of that single person, let's call him Mr. Top Dog, to provide answers, encouragement, ideas, and direction is fundamental to the company achieving early success. Unfortunately, however, all major decision-making, problems, and responsibilities seem to gravitate to Mr. Top Dog, and he relishes that situation, perhaps even has things structured so it can be no other way. Everyone else is paralyzed, afraid to act independently even within their specific areas of responsibility. People, decisions, problems—everything has to wait for Mr. Top Dog's decision. And so, the company encounters its first internal problem—a leadership crisis. The company has created a major stumbling block to its ability to succeed and grow. Mr. Top Dog becomes a limiting factor, stifling the ability of the company to progress and grow beyond the limits of what one person, no matter how competent, can possibly handle.

Making the First Adjustment

Mr. Top Dog finally learns that for the well-being of the company he must delegate authority and responsibility to others. Reluctantly, he gives in to the inevitable and issues general plans and broad policies through which he wants the company to be directed. The other members of the management group enthusiastically accept their broader responsibilities and relish their newfound executive freedom and authority. Cautious at first, Mr. Top Dog keeps a close eye on progress, and the company starts to grow again. Mr. Top Dog smiles and starts taking short vacations.

What's Going on Here?

One day Mr. Top Dog discovers that the company now has 400 employees, opened a new branch sales office last month in Buffalo, and bought a new computer and network system for the accounting department at a cost of $50,000. It also has three active but incomplete versions of the employees handbook, is studying the possibilities of contracting out all of its machine shop work, and has started an engineering project to upgrade its third most popular product.

"What's going on here?" Mr. Top Dog cries out. "Who approved all this? I didn't."

Mr. Top Dog has just discovered the next major disaster stage—a loss of control. This loss of control does not necessarily mean the company has become unprofitable or is in financial difficulty. In fact, the awareness of a loss of control probably comes earlier if the company actually gets into financial trouble.

"We can't run a company this way," Mr. Top Dog announces. "We need some controls around here. We've got to work together before we grow ourselves into bankruptcy."

And so the company reviews and improves all its systems, controls, and procedures, in the process discovering that it had far outgrown what it had originally installed some time ago. In fact, Mr. Top Dog shakes his head in amazement that the company has made it this far without a disaster. He asks for more detailed reports, formal requisitions, review committees, approval committees, authorization committees. Realizing he doesn't have the time to review and approve everything, he gives specific dollar authority to certain executives or to executive committees within the context of quarterly or annual allocation grants. Only summary reports and condensations will be reviewed by Mr. Top Dog. Mr. Top Dog is certain he can now sleep more soundly.

The Bureaucratic Jungle

Time passes, and one day the Vice-President of Sales, Mr. Hot Shot, comes into Mr. Top Dog's office and pounds his fist on the desk. "Boss, I've been trying to get that new branch service office started in Phoenix for six weeks and I've been beating my head against the wall. Big Customer Inc. has threatened to cancel their million-dollar order if I don't set up that local service office across from their Phoenix plant."

Mr. Top Dog straightens out the sterling-silver pen and pencil set on his desk and replies, "Calm down now, Hot. What's the hold-up? I thought you and I both agreed to go ahead."

"It's the system, Boss. I've been trying to get all the requisitions prepared for the Capital Equipment Review Committee, but it needs three competitive quotes for every item over $500.00. There must be a hundred of those. Personnel won't let me advertise for servicemen until they do a wage-and-benefit survey, and that's not scheduled to be completed until next week. Now the Controller's office just reminded me that I'm supposed to send the office lease to the company lawyer for review before it can be signed. I'm going nuts with all this paperwork, Boss."

Rubbing his chin in thought, Mr. Top Dog asks, "Can't they expedite things? Take a few shortcuts? Help you out?"

Mr. Top Dog is now learning that the price to be paid for installing a complete set of organizational systems and controls is more red tape and bureaucracy.

A Helping Hand

The need for adequate systems and controls cannot be avoided, but it is possible to reduce, and perhaps eliminate, much of the delay they cause. When a company gets to a size where communication among executives is confined to memos and forms, it's in trouble. The answer lies in teamwork and mutual assistance through *interdepartmental* cooperation and communication. If each executive knows what is going on in other departments—their priorities, problems, and needs—organizational response time can be reduced.

Good management means encouraging personal contact and interchange among executives. They should meet regularly and discuss important company matters. The meetings should always be nonconfrontational. Mr. Top Dog must be the prime mover in encouraging this cooperative and collaborative behavior.

Rites of Passage

The situations described above are typical, and it is the rare company that escapes any of them if it remains in business long enough to grow. Perhaps each situation is really inevitable, sort of a rites of passage a company must go through on the way to being successful. The best thing to do is to recognize these rites of passage as early as possible so you can do something about them before the company suffers serious harm. Remain on the alert for the symptoms, especially those that are a direct result of your own actions or style. These may be the most difficult of all for you to detect.

Analyzing an organization's problems is a process that should always start at the top. Then, after some honest soul-searching and review, you can proceed step by step down the chain of command, with each level applying the same high standards along the way.

Chapter 4
Leadership

THE clothes may be a dark blue pinstripe suit and paisley tie instead of a uniform with stars and ribbons, but the wearer in each case is a combat leader. Both individuals are engaged in a struggle with competing entities. On the one hand is the senior partner of an aggressive, respected advertising agency about to solicit a major new client; on the other hand is a two-star general responsible for the seaborne assault on an enemy-held island. The problems each leader faces in these two seemingly disparate situations are similar and far outweigh any differences that might exist. Both leaders are in a competitive situation. They may, in fact, both be fighting for the very survival of their organization.

Whether you are the head of a prestigious ad agency or the owner and head pharmacist of a neighborhood drugstore, you are engaged in business warfare, a struggle for the continued survival and prosperity of your business. Make no bones about it, running a business is tough. It requires a variety of talents, personal characteristics, and attitudes to be a successful leader. It isn't always pleasant; it can get rough and is an enormous challenge.

THE PRINCIPLES OF WAR

According to David J. Rogers in *Waging Business Warfare*, the eight principles of war are also applicable to winning in the competitive world of business:

1. Maintaining the objective: Pursue your specific goals at all times. If you allow yourself or your organization to be diverted from the target, you are inviting failure.

2. Concentrating resources: Focus your organizational strengths

where you have the advantage or where your competition is most vulnerable. You have two types of opportunities—those created by your strengths and those created by your competitor's weaknesses.

3. Offensive action: You may not lose through a good defense, but you cannot win, either. At some point, to achieve victory, you must attack.

4. Mobility: Be flexible and willing to adapt to new realities. Don't always try to tackle the competition head on. Often it's easier to find the path of least resistance and press forward with all your strength.

5. Surprise: Don't let them know or be able to anticipate your next step. Take the initiative. Keep them guessing and "hit them where they ain't."

6. Security: Keep your eyes and ears open. Know what your competition is doing or thinking of doing. Knowledge is power.

7. Economy of force: Use your manpower in proportion to the objective to be reached and the problems to be faced in achieving that goal. It is better to have a few capable, "willing" people than a horde of grudging incompetents.

8. Unity of command: All the forces and resources you muster in your struggle must form a cooperative, cohesive effort. The leadership must be united and supportive of one another.

Personal Leadership: The Vital Ingredient

The quality of leadership you provide is the foundation for what happens at your company. Management's intelligence, insight, foresight, and temperament are what provide the strategy, tactics, actions, and reactions taken by the company and executed by its personnel.

A leader must be bold. He will frequently not have all the data and answers; in fact, he may not even know all the questions. Nevertheless, a good leader will possess a deep reservoir of self-confidence and optimism that permits him to be decisive.

Too often, would-be managers come out of college with their MBAs and try to make business decisions based on mathematical formulas. They are convinced there is an equation applicable to every general management decision. The truth is, formulas and equations are just another useful tool—part of the data background that a manager will use when he evaluates, weighs, considers, and processes the information before making a management decision, be it strategic or tactical.

A good leader must have a total grasp of the situation confronting his company, that is, the ability to distill the data available and arrive at the correct course of action through an intuitive process—weighing the tangibles and intangibles to arrive at the right conclusion. If it were not so, and the MBAs were right, then computers would be the presidents of companies. A classic, contemporary example is Mr. Spock of the TV show "Star Trek." Mr. Spock is a brilliant logician but is rarely capable of intuitive insight. He is a great #2 to Captain Kirk, but he's not in Kirk's league as a leader.

Even so, the bold, decisive leader remains prudent and does not allow his ego to delude him. He is realistic but is able to remain optimistic and confident in the future. Invariably, the good leader is objective, truthful, honest, and fair to employees and subordinates.

Wisdom May Be Collective, but Leadership Is Singular

Running a business is not an exercise in democracy; at best it is a benign dictatorship. There may be committee meetings, staff input, executive conferences, and so forth, but in the end there is one individual who says yes or no, turn this way or that way, go or stop. So long as that individual has been granted the authority and responsibility by the owners, stockholders, or directors, he must lead the fight and others must follow his lead.

In *Waging Business Warfare*, Rogers notes: "In every instance of great tactical success in battle, the person in command demonstrated it—a willingness to fight. No substitute exists for the initiative and resolve that exploit the other side's error or its blindness or its susceptibility to deception; or that sees and quickly seizes an opportunity that appears totally unexpectedly or that brings the opponent to battle at the time and place you desire."

A Rock-Solid Intangible

Leadership is not skin-deep. Most of us have met individuals who on the surface do not seem particularly impressive, but who have demonstrated the talent for leadership. It may have been that 98-pound weakling in high school who organized and ran those successful entertainment programs in your junior and senior year; or your neighbor, the unassuming fellow who waves to you while walking his dog, who has spearheaded the long-overdue revitalization of the township's educational program as school board president. Perhaps at your college reunion you met a fraternity brother who is now the president of a well-known multi-million-dollar public company but who barely managed to get passing grades.

The art of leadership can be learned. While your personality is important, the potential for effective leadership springs from your sense of self-confidence. Self-confidence combined with a personal winning strategy is an unbeatable combination that can inspire others to follow your lead and your orders.

A Winning Personal Strategy

Certain elements are basic to the personal strategies of those who assume the responsibilities of leadership:

1. Plan ahead and pay attention to details. There is a time and place for spontaneous decision-making and the "big-picture" look, but taking the time to plan is vital.

2. To get your subordinates to rise to the occasion, you must clearly define the company's mission. Let your people know what the plan is, and keep them informed as to how that plan is progressing.

3. Know the strengths and weaknesses of your people. It is foolhardy to put your team in a situation where they don't have the tools or abilities to be successful no matter how hard they try. By the same token, to misuse or ignore the strengths of your people is equally foolish.

4. The amount of resources you have does not make you an automatic winner; it only provides you with an opportunity to succeed. A limited amount of resources does not make you an automatic loser. You must fight the battle that best suits the resources you do have. Also, because resources are typically limited, you and your team must have the right tools to do the job at the right time.

5. You must know exactly what is happening out in the field, whether it's new technology, new customers, new competitors, or a change in economic conditions. Get out on the road yourself periodically. No matter how good your management information system is, you cannot operate by remote control. Firsthand confirmation will improve your management batting average.

6. Keep an eye on your span of control and that of your subordinates. Regardless of the size of your organization, the size of the teams must be manageable and everyone's efforts coordinated.

7. No matter how complex the undertaking, always follow the

"KISS" (Keep It Simple, Stupid) philosophy. Unfortunately, breaking down a task or endeavor into simpler components usually results in more individual components to manage and coordinate. Yet, on balance, the less complicated a task, the greater number of successes and fewer failures you will have to contend with.

8. Allowing your competition to rest or recover is an invitation to losing. You must keep the pressure on your competitors, pressing your advantage and keeping them on the defensive. Not only does that have an impact on the competition, but it keeps your own organization from losing its fighting edge and growing fat, dumb, and happy.

The simple reality is that to achieve success you must provide better leadership than your competitors. Knowledge, experience, and technology are of limited value unless they are harnessed and directed by a manager possessing and using the art of leadership.

Someone once wrote that the overall victory does not occur in one big battle, but is actually the result of a number of other victories in the component parts of the struggle against your adversary. The leader who applies that principle stands a better chance of succeeding.

Chapter 5
Organization

ALTHOUGH you probably have difficult days when you have serious doubts, for better or worse your company is an organization. Perhaps you haven't issued formal organization charts with neat rectangles and straight lines connecting the different boxes, but if your company employs more than one person, you have some form of an organization. Titles, boxes, and lines alone, however, do not make an organization. The process is much more subtle—and difficult. It is also continuous. As manager, you have no one to blame but yourself when your organization fails to achieve its corporate objectives.

Hail, Hail, the Gang's All Here

Included among the definitions of an organization are "an administrative structure arranged by systematic planning and united effort, formed into a coherent unity or functioning whole." If your company matches that definition, you have a lot for which to be thankful. Unfortunately, many companies skip a word or two in the development of their organization—words like "systematic planning," "coherent unity," "functioning whole." In that case, perhaps you really are the "leader of the gang." No one really intends for that to happen, certainly not Mr. Alfred, president and board chairman of Alfred Designs, Inc.

Mr. Alfred was a brilliant, creative design engineer who started as an independent consultant and soon had developed a large clientele. Several snack food companies regularly contracted for his services to design mechanisms and assemblies to package their brand-name products. As the business grew, Mr. Alfred hired a few draftsmen and recent engineering graduates to lay out and draft his designs. He provided direct leadership and continued to be the primary contact with customers. Financial records were maintained by an outside public accountant, and the limited administrative and clerical work was handled by an experienced secretary and one clerk. The consulting practice continued to grow, and Mr. Alfred hired more engineers and draftsmen, organizing them on a project basis.

In less than ten years, Alfred Designs Inc. had seventy-five employees, all well compensated, including five supervising engineers (reporting to Mr. Alfred), sixty-five engineers and draftsmen reporting to the supervisory engineers, and five administrative personnel under the direction of the secretary. Billing revenues were close to $4 million a year.

At this point Alfred Designs was forced to make a significant change in the way it did business. Customers now insisted that the company build and deliver completed, working systems, instead of providing just blueprints and drawings. The company was now in the manufacturing business, an entirely new discipline for Mr. Alfred and most of his personnel.

Mr. Alfred assumed that the new manufacturing responsibilities would be handled exactly as the engineering work had been handled in the past: each project team would arrange for its own parts procurement, machine-shop work, and assembly. Almost immediately, purchase orders were being issued by five different project groups working on eleven different customer orders. The company soon found that designing something on paper was a far cry from assembling it. When one young engineer disclosed a talent for putting things together, he was "borrowed" by other project teams to lead the assembly work. A draftsman with the least design and drawing experience became the unofficial purchasing agent for several project teams. Through inexperience, he usually paid too much for most items.

Mr. Alfred remained detached from the new activities, preferring to concentrate on new business development and design review, the things he enjoyed doing.

Sometime later, as many projects fell further behind schedule and the company began to run short of cash, Mr. Alfred suspected he had a problem. No one seemed to be in charge. His five supervisory engineers seemed to be running five different competing companies. Project leaders were scrambling for the same resources—retaining personnel after projects were completed, sequestering common inventory items, and claiming more and more of the company's limited manufacturing space. In short, Alfred Designs Inc. was suffering from a severe case of anarchy and disorganization.

Fortunately, Mr. Alfred asserted himself in time to save the company when two of his long-standing clients, frustrated with late delivery and poor manufacturing, canceled their orders.

*

Rather than plan a structure, many managers allow the company to sort itself out as it proceeds on its merry way. Some general guidelines may be issued and major turf boundaries honored, but for the most part, the organization takes it shape and structure in knee-jerk response to inside or outside stimuli. The inevitable result: fuzzy lines of authority, the rumblings of anarchy here and there, some large gaps in accountability, a lack of checks and balances with poor internal controls, managers and other employees who are square pegs in round holes, and a chaotic approach to anticipating and solving the problems of running the business.

THE IDEAL ORGANIZATION: FICTION OR FACT?

Harvey Sherman is quoted as having said, "There is no one 'ideal' or 'best' organization except for a particular agency, at a particular time, with particular people, and . . . even then, the best organization can only be best for some purposes and some people, while at the same time being less than the best for other purposes and other people."

What this means is that the organizational structure of most companies is a compromise, and probably far from an ideal compromise at that. The company is faced with a multidimensional dilemma: the executives suggest one format; the needs of the corporation demand a different format; the owner/manager feels more comfortable with a third format; and, to top it off, the future will demand another format.

Although most organization charts should probably be written in pencil, the reality is that most businesses cannot deal with the trauma and dislocation of constant reorganization. The experts say that every organization is composed of four basic parts—people, tasks, management, and environment, none of which is a constant. Your challenge is to mold and sustain an organization that can remain resilient and flexible enough to handle the inevitable changes in the four basic parts, yet still be able to achieve its goals through a cooperative and efficient effort.

You will not find the perfect organization for your company in any textbook, because no one company is like any other company no matter how similar their products, their market, or their problems. What you can get are a few ideas about how others think they have solved their problems, at least for the time being. In the most complex effort of "organizing" your organization, certain principles can be useful.

ORGANIZATION FUNDAMENTALS

When an organization is formed, the various resources of the company, including people, are arranged to achieve certain end results. "Division of labor" is the usual term applied to the arranging of people; and that "division" is done either on the basis of the "tasks" (the work to be accomplished) or "authority" (who will be in charge of the work effort). However, you must not treat tasks and authority as unrelated considerations. People perform quite well when they know the tasks assigned to them (what to do and how to do it), but they should know under whose authority they will be working—who's the boss; who is making sure they do the job right; who will be the one that influences their raises and performance reviews?

YES SIR, YES SIR

One of the worst situations that can exist in an organization is for an employee (be it officer or assembler) or department to think it has more than one boss. Nothing is more disruptive. No one intends for this to happen, but it usually develops because a situation is allowed to continue unchecked. In general, failure to define the primary areas of responsibility among the various departments and their managers will leave the door open to usurping of authority by the managers with more aggressive, assertive personalities. Disregarding the chain of command leads to organizational chaos.

Two typical examples:

1. One manager fails to communicate through his direct subordinate, choosing instead to deal directly and continuously with that subordinate's personnel.

2. A member of one management area (finance, for example) will give orders and directions to members of another area (the sales department, for example) without communicating with and obtaining the acceptance and authorization of the second area's manager (the sales manager).

Special situations exist where an organization is deliberately designed to permit an individual or group to regularly function under more than one "boss." So-called matrix organizations permit an individual, group of individuals, or entire departments to be assigned to a basic functional department and, at the same time, assigned to work on a particular project, product, or other task under different leadership than that of their basic functional department. Even in more traditional organizations, resource centers (typing pools, drafting pools, special engineering or design talents) may be shared by or lent to more than one department at a time. Unless the ground rules have been clearly delineated for how the matrix or resource sharing systems will function, including responsibility for work output, prioritization, performance reviews, and compensation, you may find yourself with frustrated supervisors and unhappy employees.

Not surprisingly, many CEOs are the most frequent perpetrators of bypassing or short-circuiting the chain of command. Somehow, from their lofty positions, they feel empowered to swoop in anywhere and anytime they choose, leaving the authority and reputation of their executives in ruins, employees constantly looking over their shoulder, and an organization immobilized by fear. A better way for senior executives to conduct themselves is to work *with* and *through* the organization structure, not around it.

Delegating Authority: Sharing the Burden

There are several laws of nature that an executive cannot refute: You can't be in two places at once, and there is only one of you. It follows, then, that your company's ability to grow and prosper is directly related to your ability to share authority with your subordinate executives. Delegating authority, and with it the responsibility for results and performance, is the essence of organization and executive competence.

Your subordinates must be allowed to share in decision-making appropriate to their respective levels and spheres in the organization. Within certain areas, the subordinate executive must have the right to act on his or her own discretion and initiative. In other areas, the executive may be limited to making recommendations that then require peer-executive approval before taking effect. In every instance, however, the delegation of authority must be preceded by a clear and complete job description. In addition, subordinates must understand the various organizational relationships, including those beyond their immediate boundaries.

Chapter 6

Intracompany Warfare

EVERY day, vicious hostilities take place that are costly, demoralizing, and dangerous to the health and prosperity of the companies in which they occur, including yours.

A surprising number of executives turn a blind eye and a deaf ear to such goings-on in the mistaken belief that competition and controversy is healthy and keeps personnel on its toes. An equally large number of executives actually encourages, aids, and abets those destructive practices because of ego and "my turf" considerations, or because they have a misguided understanding of their own role and mission.

Within a company, battles can be waged both within departments and between departments. Never allow any battle to gain a foothold. It is difficult enough to survive and prosper in today's highly competitive business climate, let alone having to worry about internal competition and hostility.

SALES VS. THE CREDIT AND COLLECTIONS DEPARTMENT

One of the more common struggles in a business is between the sales department, who thinks every customer deserves unlimited credit and/or time to pay invoices, and the credit department, who thinks most customers are deadbeats who refuse to or can't pay their bills on time.

The major difficulty is that the two departments are usually measured according to different objectives: for sales, the increase in sales volume and new accounts opened; for credit, minimization of bad-debt losses and reduction in collection time. While these objectives are important, they must be measured in the context of other realities. For example, a sale is a loss if you don't get paid, and restrictive credit practices can stifle sales growth or lose customers.

The granting of credit is a tool that must be used in conjunction with selling activities; a working partnership in which there is mutual respect for each other's function.

In a judgment-call situation, most small and mid-size companies tend to lean toward credit liberalization. That's okay, provided the credit department knows the rationale. When a decision is made against granting credit, sales management and the salesman must be given the background details and data to support the decision. Perhaps together, credit and sales can work out special terms to permit the sale while minimizing the collection risk. A credit department that is given the opportunity to participate in the development of creative solutions to difficult sales situations is usually one with a high morale and good overall performance rating.

Senior management can create the environment for this cooperative spirit. Among the factors necessary are:

- A respect for the basic role of each party
- A balanced approach to each party's concerns
- Regular review by the sales manager of the aged accounts-receivable trial balance
- Participation by the credit manager in sales meetings, trade shows, visits to customers, and other sales department activities
- Guidelines regarding credit approval, terms, and procedures that are mandatory reading for both credit and sales personnel

Some companies have eliminated many potential disputes beforehand by automatically allowing a reasonable dollar limit of open credit to any new customer on their first order. The amount of such credit is a function of the size of the company granting credit, the price of its products, and the degree of risk management is willing to take without a detailed, prior investigation. Such a policy permits a fast approval response from the credit department and considerable ease in opening new accounts for the sales force. You should evaluate the wisdom of such a policy based on your company's own financial and market considerations.

Manufacturing vs. Engineering

"The bills of material are wrong and incomplete" is the usual cry from manufacturing management when a production problem arises. "They can't follow directions; they don't know what they're doing" is the response from engineering management. Meanwhile, thousands of dollars are being wasted, deliveries are being missed, and customers are getting impatient. Sound familiar? It's a regular event at many so-called technology companies.

The classic confrontation relates to the process of releasing to manufacturing a new product or a substantially redesigned product model. More than likely, unforeseen engineering problems or market changes have caused engineeıing to be months, maybe a year, late in completing the design. Several prototypes have been hand-built and field-tested, but the design may still contain some bugs. Last-minute drawing changes are still being made; in fact, there's a backlog. The quality assurance department is clamoring for more changes while the marketing department is screaming that any further delay will cost the company its market. At some early point in this process, the purchasing department was given the go-ahead to order "long-lead-time" parts and components so that manufacturing could start production.

With recent engineering changes, some items are no longer needed or will require extensive reworking. Few, if any, of the regular manufacturing personnel know how to put the new product together correctly or efficiently. Chaos and confusion abound. What a way to run a business!

Of all the activities of a manufacturing company, none is so expensive, time-consuming, and aggravating as the "new product release syndrome." It is undoubtedly one of the most complex undertakings that a business organization goes through, and few companies do it well. The more successful companies approach this area of potential conflict using the "Five P Formula":

- Planning
- Partnership
- Procedures
- Performance
- Patience

Planning

1. Try to anticipate the ordinary and extraordinary problems that will arise in accomplishing the objective.

2. Allow sufficient time for the activity, recognizing that significant delays in the engineering phase cannot fully be made up by reducing the time allotted for quality assurance or manufacturing.

3. Establish a series of date and dollar benchmarks where the project will be reviewed and reassessed. Advise personnel of those benchmarks when the project is started.

Partnership

1. Assign manufacturing and quality assurance personnel to the engineering team as early in the process as possible. The value of their input regarding requirements and practices on the manufacturing floor will have time- and money-saving value to the engineering personnel.

2. Designate some of the engineering personnel working on the design to be the liaisons who will transfer to the manufacturing department when the design is released for production. Those engineering personnel will have more detailed knowledge of the new product, as well as the ability to provide in-depth instruction and recommend solutions.

Procedures

1. Codify and distribute to all departments exact procedures for such activities as engineering change requests; purchase order approval, preparation and release; and test specifications.

2. Issue specific instructions regarding the structure and organization of the bill of materials, blueprint and drawing standards, and parts and component specifications.

Performance

1. Review regularly the performance of the engineering personnel in budgeted and elapsed time, as well as their adherence to the product design objectives.

2. Test the operation of the prototype models and their component assemblies for meeting the performance objectives. Did they do what they were supposed to do?

3. Revalidate the projected standard cost of the product. Are the

original estimates of manufacturing cost and gross profit margins still valid?

4. Monitor the performance of, and problems encountered by, the manufacturing department as they integrate the new product into the normal production operations.

5. Observe closely what is happening at the customers who are acting as "beta test" sites, or who have received early shipments of the new product. Remain alert for signs of failures, defects, or customer disappointment.

Patience

1. Learn when to push and when to ease off. Constant pressure on engineering and/or manufacturing can result in their taking short-cuts, which could result in even larger, more expensive problems for the company.

2. The gestation process for a new product is closer to an art form than an exact science. Mistakes will be made, but they should be used as a learning experience for the next time.

The "Five P formula" can be adapted to a number of special interdepartmental activities, such as the development and installation of a new computer and management information system, or the implementation of an employee performance review and evaluation system.

Accounting vs. Everyone Else

In most organizations the accounting department usually has the worst interdepartmental relations. Frequently looked upon as "useless overhead" by those who design, produce, or sell the company's products, the accountants are the "bean-counters" and "pencil-pushers."

Part of the negative feelings stem from one of the basic functions of the accounting department personnel: They are the scorekeepers. They record and add up the results of everyone's efforts and publish the final tally. The figures don't lie: "Your department is over budget by 12 percent," or "This expense report is incorrect," or "Manufacturing overhead is too high."

Unfortunately, in many companies, the leadership of the accounting department usually doesn't help overcome this attitude. It may even seem to revel in it and seek to remain aloof from the rest of the company.

Rather than trying to function as an active team player, the department makes no real effort to learn about the problems and pressures faced by the other departments of the company. Management and personnel of the other departments react in kind. Departments try to outwit the accounting system. The overall effect is to cheat the company of a valuable asset—the integration of the knowledge, training, and capabilities of the accounting department into a working partnership with the rest of the company.

The accounting department is in a unique position to provide an overall perspective on the company's activities. The fact that they are not part of the actual "operations" of the company (in terms of designing, producing, and selling) enables them to provide valuable insights and suggestions.

How do you achieve that objective? To start with, it is a "top-down" process. Your accounting department must see its mission as more than standing on the sidelines as the scorekeeper. But also, the CEO and COO of the company must encourage the management of the accounting department to be an active, constructive participant in the creation, development, and execution of the company's business plan. If the CEO and COO set the example for the rest of the executive management group, then the accounting department's relationships, self-esteem, and contributions will improve considerably, to the collective benefit of the entire company.

There is no doubt that the solution starts at the top, but you must first make certain that your accounting leadership has the ability to rise to the occasion and become more than "bean-counters." If you do not believe they can, then find people who will be able to do so. Your company cannot afford to be without it.

Chapter 7

It's My Company

MOST entrepreneurs work long hours in an unstructured environment, putting their heart and soul into their businesses to make the dream come true. They ignore personal wants and desires in the struggle to make the fledgling business successful. Understandably, a serious business problem can trigger an overwhelming parental instinct in a founder, but that instinct itself unfortunately may generate destructive behavior that could result in disaster.

A classic conflict often arising at time of crisis in both public and privately owned small to mid-sized firms is the animosity that erupts between the original founder and the members of the executive staff hired while the company was in its growth phase. The situation develops frequently in high-tech companies, but it is by no means unique to that type of industry; any company may fall victim under certain circumstances. It is also common in family-owned and managed companies, where a father or uncle has turned over day-to-day management to younger family members.

A DIFFERENT SET OF VALUES

One basis for the conflict is the founder's intense emotional attachment to the company, which the newer employees simply can't match, even if they are the founder's relatives. At times of crisis, the founder will work whatever hours are necessary to overcome the emergency. Anyone who does any less may be considered disloyal by the founder. Just when the strain of events demands absolute cooperation, the founder's behavior generates unjustified rancor and bitterness. The inevitable results are scars and bruised egos that will hamper the ongoing relationship.

THE PAST IS NOT THE PRESENT

A founder's unfamiliarity with or refusal to follow the company's present systems and procedures is disruptive. As a company evolves, it inevitably becomes more formalized, with departments, procedures, delegation of authority, and the other trappings of growth. A founder may find himself baffled by the new infrastructure when he tries to accomplish everything by fiat, tactics that will no longer work in the current organization. A founder who suddenly steps in at an operational level after being inactive in a day-to-day role will clash head on with the well-established momentum, or inertia, of the company infrastructure.

In a high-tech company, the founder may want to reprioritize the work of engineers, scientists, technicians, and model-makers; reschedule manufacturing; and commandeer all the company's technical resources. He may also want to bypass all normal systems, including engineering-change notices, quality-assurance tests, and the like. Moreover, in a world of rapidly changing technology, the founder may have lost touch and failed to keep up. This only fuels the conflict.

For thirty years, Kooltest Controls Corporation manufactured a full line of temperature controls used by industrial furnace manufacturers in their products. Under Joshua Albert, its founder and first engineer, the company developed a respected reputation for expertise in using precision shaped and formed bimetallic pieces to maintain accurate high temperatures in both gas and electrically-heated furnaces and kilns. Five years ago, Mr. Albert delegated day-to-day operational control to a new president of his choosing, but retained a part-time position as board chairman.

Recently, orders began to drop off sharply as more and more customers switched to semiconductor technology instead of bimetallics. These new controllers were accurate, cheaper and more reliable. While the company continued to supply bimetallic temperature controllers as replacement parts, these were no longer the industry standard.

Mr. Albert, who knew little about semiconductors, rejected the advice of the company president and senior marketing and engineering executives to upgrade to semiconductor technology. Instead, he insisted the company continue to concentrate on further development of the company's now-obsolete bimetallics.

Soon, dissatisfied with progress, he fired the top engineering manager and assumed leadership of the research department. As more orders were lost to competitive products, Mr. Albert futilely tried to achieve the impossible with out-of-date technology. The president and many of the younger engineers resigned.

Mr. Albert then resumed total day-to-day control of the company. Within two years, he had lost a major portion of the executive and engineering staff and was suffering significant operating losses. Mr. Albert sold what was left of his company for slightly over book value and retired.

*

In the drive to meet a new challenge threatening his company, a founder may take a bold technological step forward to regain competitiveness or retreat with the battle cry, "Let's do it like we did in the old days," which is an invitation to disaster. The fact is that no company today can successfully operate in the same manner as it did in years gone by: a reality many founders fail to recognize or somehow ignore in their ill-fated ride to the rescue.

A Time for Maturity

How can you avoid or at least minimize problems and conflicts when they occur? If you and your management team sit down and discuss the possibility of such conflicts well before a bad situation develops, everyone will be "presensitized" and thus able to have direct, open discussions later on, before tempers reach the boiling point and everyone becomes deaf to the "other side."

Sometimes, the crisis can be isolated from the normal operations of the company and lessen the disruption of daily routines. Then you can step into a more active role without causing damage. It's always good management practice to isolate major problems from the rest of the organization. This permits you to objectively assess the parameters of the problem and find appropriate solutions.

The best approach is probably the most difficult of all: Keep out of it. Unless you have lost confidence in your management team, there is no reason for you to jump in with both feet. If ever there is a time for mature leadership and support, it is during a time of crisis.

Papa Knows Best

Family-owned and managed companies often have another set of problems that simmer under the surface, erupt periodically, then are patched over for a while. Usually such situations involve a father bringing one or more children into the business, siblings being in business together, or a combination of both. Having relatives in ownership and management positions places enormous burdens on the already complex and delicate management/employee relationship. The normal frictions between co-workers become almost impossible to leave at the office at five o'clock. They resurface at family holidays, celebrations, and events. Parents, spouses, children, and other family members get drawn into the conflict and relatives take sides. Where the family should be a source of support, it soon becomes an extended battlefield. This can be a painful, stressful situation for everyone directly and indirectly involved.

Getting Professional Help

No one in the family should attempt to resolve a company dispute. They can only make things worse, no matter how well-meaning they might be.

Now is the time to consult a business psychologist, who as a trained professional is better equipped to deal effectively with such situations. They can remain objective to the company's needs, yet still be sensitive to the underlying family dynamics. Often, the dispute may have less to do with a difference in business judgment and tactics than with other normal but deep-seated emotional pressures of long standing. In fact, it would be best if professional help were obtained as early as possible, preferably at the time the family member is brought into the business. A qualified professional will be able to alert the principles to the potential conflicts and dangers and set up a methodology everyone can use to avoid or at least minimize the problems. Family relationships and business relationships should be able to co-exist, but it may not always be easy.

PART 2

Basic Business Management

HOW does a company become a well-oiled, efficient money-making machine? It doesn't happen very often, and it isn't easy to accomplish or sustain; otherwise, every business would be a success and none would ever fail. Business operations and performance can be improved by taking care of basic factors that managers frequently overlook or give short shrift to. For the most part, these factors are within the power of the individual manager to shape and control. Address yourself to how well it can be done.

Chapter 8

Planning

LEADERSHIP, as vital as it is, is only one tool of management. Leadership deals with how people will behave, while management encompasses the use of *all* resources in an organization—money, plant, equipment, processes, materials, *and* people. Each of us may know someone who can lead but is ineffective at some or several management activities—planning, organizing, staffing, directing, coordinating, or controlling. The first and perhaps most important management activity is planning.

Being Small Can Be a Plus

One advantage a small businessman has over the executive of a large firm is the shorter distance between him and the problems of the business. While it is true that executives of a large business usually have more resources (personnel, assets, and time) to draw upon, the successful small businessman should be quicker to detect a problem because he is closer to the actual battleground. An unsolved or undetected problem doesn't have to wend its way up the organizational ladder. What's more, in the larger organization, problem identification and analysis is subject to distortions because of the "whisper-down-the-lane" effect of each corporate level.

But being small is a double-edged sword. A smaller organization is usually more vulnerable and less likely to survive the impact of its problems. With fewer resources, the manager of a small business must be constantly on the alert for trouble in any area of his business's activities.

While a small businessman may have a particular strength in engineering, sales, manufacturing, or other management specialty, he must be a generalist too, and direct the total scope of the company's operations, including those for which he has no particular training or experience.

How, then, does the small business manager get to know what should happen, what has happened, and what will happen? The answer lies with the multiple but related processes of planning and measuring results, as well as with feedback from all segments of the business. From top down or bottom up, a business needs a strategic plan. But even before you develop a strategic plan, you must establish your company's long-term goals and objectives.

What Do You Want to Be?

Not every businessman wants to run a "big" business. The corner pharmacist may be satisfied with just one modest, but profitable, store. He doesn't seek to become another CVS multilocation semi-department-store chain. The owner of a fifty-employee tool and die shop may not want to become the $20-million-a-year supplier of precision jet-aircraft components to Lockheed. The point is, before you start the planning process, you must decide how "big" you want to be and how soon you want to get there.

Your long-term goals are the context within which you will develop your strategic plan. Even if the opportunities for rapid, dynamic growth are available to you, if growth is not your objective, then you will be making different decisions within the same set of circumstances that another executive with a more ambitious set of goals would make.

You must resolve some personal matters and priorities before you embark on the business plan. These include such things as how hard you want to work, your family situation, age, and health. By tackling these issues first, you will be better prepared to structure your business plan and avoid some of the pressures of future events. Before you set objectives for your company, do some soul-searching and set some for yourself.

Basic Strategic Planning

Every business, from the local card and gift shop to the builder of supersonic aircraft, must be run according to a plan. Many books are available to help you learn the strategic planning process. The principles of the process are essentially the same for large businesses and small.

In its simplest fashion, a strategic business plan forecasts the future (including assumptions), finds and assesses present and future opportunities and obstacles, chooses a course of action, and then prepares detailed action plans that show what management and employees must do to take advantage of that future.

A strategic plan is a plan for survival as well as a plan for improvement. Not all events that affect a business come as a total surprise. A business that is constantly buffeted about by unforeseen circumstances is a business in which management has been doing no strategic planning or, at best, is planning poorly. Only the luckiest business can survive and prosper without adequate strategic planning.

What Is Strategic Planning?

Strategy is the art of understanding an anticipated situation or environment and determining how best to adapt to it. Because strategic planning tends to deal with the less defined, less certain aspects of a present or future situation, it follows that the strategies thus developed will have to be relatively broad in scope.

Robert J. Mockler in his book, *Business Planning and Policy Formulation*, defines business planning as "an intellectual process which requires analyzing anticipated future circumstances, both external (environmental) and internal (company), and developing within the context of that future a company objective, guidelines for action (policies), implementation plans, an organization, and controls designed to achieve the objective."

Strategic planning is like making decisions today with tomorrow and tomorrow's objectives in mind. A strategic plan is absolutely essential for a business, but it doesn't have to be cast in concrete. It must, however, be regularly revalidated, updated, and modified. While the plan is a compass that holds the organization on course, the winds and weather of reality may require some course adjustments along the way.

The Components of a Strategic Plan

In addition to defining your corporate goals and objectives, you will include a series of policies and directives, resource requirements and allocations, and an integrated and organized system of financial budgets and projections.

Budgets and projections are statements of expected results expressed in financial and/or numerical terms. As tools used in the planning process, these budgets and forecasts are vital. Unfortunately, many managers give them short shrift, preferring instead to consign them to the accountants. In reality, the budgets and forecasts should be developed and prepared by department managers and executives with the assistance of accounting personnel. Every manager should be personally responsible for the preparation of the budgets and forecasts of his group. The failure of a manager to do so is an indication that he may not understand or accept the plan.

Budgets: The Yardsticks of Progress

The use of operating budgets, capital budgets, long- and short-term cash forecasts, and other financial projections provide a basis for measuring progress (or the lack of progress) in achieving your objectives. They enable management to monitor the ever-changing situation, validate original assumptions, and spot trouble as early as possible. Without budgets and forecasts, even if the company prepares regular reports of actual results, management has only one hand on the steering wheel and one eye closed.

Chapter 9

Budgets

IF strategic planning is a foundation for achieving future success, then budgeting—the strategic plan expressed in financial terms—is also fundamental for achieving success. Initially, the budget can indicate whether or not the strategic plan is do-able within the current operating and financial structure. Budgets are also fundamental to assuring the long-term survival of your company.

No business is too small or too large to prepare the budget package. If you do not prepare a comprehensive budget to assist you and your executives in managing the business, you are overlooking an essential management tool. A budget allows you to measure actual performance. Without a budget for comparison, a report of actual results is only a series of abstract numbers. There is a big difference between merely *reporting* performance and actually *measuring* performance.

The Components of a Budget

A budget must be sufficiently detailed to cover all areas of the company and permit subsequent in-depth comparisons and analysis. It should include the following components:

1. Operating budget (P&L)
    - Sales plan (by product and/or territory)
    - Costs and expenses (by department and/or category)
    - Gross profit projection (by product and/or factory)
    - Production/inventory plan (by product and/or factory)
    - Hiring/manpower plan (by department and/or job title)
    - Incoming order forecast (by product and/or territory)

2. Capital budget
    - Asset purchases (what and when)
    - Major repairs or maintenance (what and when)
3. Cash flow forecast
    - Source and use of funds
    - Working capital changes and needs
    - Long-term capital needs
    - Borrowing or other financing activities

Organize the various budgets to flow from and coordinate with the "chart of accounts" the accounting department uses in keeping the actual books, ledgers, and journals. This permits an easier comparison of actual results. The same is true for the budget structure and the company's organization structure. You should be able to superimpose the organization chart of the company (with all executives and their departments) over the budget and then match each manager's area of executive responsibility and authority with his area's costs and expenses in the budget. Each manager should be able to identify, understand, and have primary control over every portion of the budget for which he will be held responsible.

THE OPERATING BUDGET

An oversimplified characterization of the operating budget is to say it's a "forecasted P & L." It is certainly that and much more. When you and the members of the management team are preparing an operating budget, you are actually constructing a model of the company's anticipated operations element by element. In addition to establishing "how much it will cost," you are also asking "Why should it cost us?" and "Are we getting fair value?" The process of budget preparation is a far better teacher than any business book.

A lazy manager may use actual numbers from some prior period as a "quasi-budget" with which to compare current or future performance. While this is better than having no budget at all, using last month's or last year's numbers to evaluate current performance probably means you are not working toward your business plan.

For example, suppose you spent $3,000 for overtime premium in the first quarter of last year but only $2,000 this quarter. This does not necessarily mean progress or improvement. There are too many unanswered questions, such as: What is the relationship between the overtime premium cost and your planned rate of production or employment level? Had you prepared a complete operating budget, the amount of overtime premium budgeted would have been a subset of the planned production, hiring level, and/or sales for this quarter.

THE CAPITAL BUDGET

A strategic plan may require a company to purchase capital equipment, acquire real estate, make expensive repairs and improvements, or other such significant asset-acquisition actions. Some of those actions may be contingent upon the accomplishment of other events or steps in the strategic plan. Accordingly, the capital budget is the summary, authorization, and timetable for all such capital expenditures. Given that significant dollars may be involved in the capital budget, it forms an essential part of the strategic plan and can have a major impact upon your downstream cash requirements, which will then be reflected in your cash flow forecast.

THE CASH FLOW FORECAST

Although often omitted in the budgeting systems of many companies, the cash flow forecast is an important piece of management data. A properly prepared cash flow forecast can predict the size of a potential financial crisis sufficiently in advance to permit management to take the necessary corrective action. Moreover, the development of the cash flow forecast and the information it presents can highlight problems in your accounts-receivable collection processes, or affect your capital-equipment purchase program, dividend policy, borrowing or equity plans. Since it is the lack of cash that usually signals the downfall of most companies, every company, with or without a strategic plan, *must* prepare a regular and timely cash flow forecast.

SETTING A BUDGETING HORIZON

Although the strategic plan should cover a period of several years (and be reviewed and recast at least once a year thereafter), the detailed budget package derived from the strategic plan normally covers only the next twelve-month period, broken down by months and/or quarters. Depending upon the complexity of the budget, the staff available, and the financial vulnerability of the company, many firms use a "rolling" twelve-month budget, updating the current budget every quarter and moving it out three more months. Quarterly budgets are probably sufficient, provided the company makes full use of the weekly "key data" reports, as described in Chapter 10.

Frequently, a company misuses budget data when comparing actual results because it tries to divide a thirteen-week quarter by three to arrive at a correct month's value. There are four-week months and five-week months, and categories such as sales, payroll, payroll taxes, and utility costs, will be distorted if such differences aren't acknowledged. Ideally, when breaking down a quarterly budget into a shorter time period, recast each budget item by its own appropriate time factor.

Other Benefits of Budgeting

The budgeting process forces management to establish monetary and other types of targets that are developed from and based upon the planned course of company action over a specific time frame. Almost every item on a profit-and-loss statement can be reasonably predicted on the basis of one or more elements of your business plan for the period. You and the rest of the management team must set the appropriate expenditure level for all expenses and costs within the context of a revenue and/or production plan, and the anticipated financial condition of the company.

By preparing a budget, you and your managers will gain immeasurable insight regarding the costs of doing business. Just a few of the things you will learn are such matters as what it takes to keep the organization going; the realities of fixed, semivariable, and variable expenses; and the financial consequences of management action or inaction. Budgeting is an excellent tool for building and training better, more effective management.

Chapter 10

Management Information

THE level of timely financial information available to company executives fluctuates from one extreme to another and is not a function of the size of the corporation. Some small companies must wait for monthly or quarterly visits from their CPA (usually well *after* the end of the accounting period) and fly blind the rest of the time. At best, the business manager has only a checkbook balance to use as a status report. In other small companies, the manager may pour forth a never-ending stream of information and minutiae of dubious value from his personal computer. Similar situations exist in larger corporations, too. Company size is no guarantee of the financial data's quality, timeliness, or usefulness.

The Scorecard

Financial reports in all their configurations serve a number of purposes. But do the traditional monthly financial reports—balance sheet, profit-and-loss (operating) statement, and the statement of changes in financial position—really tell management what it needs to know? Probably not. The bankers may like to see them, and so too the stockholders, but those reports alone rarely provide management with the best information in the most useful format.

It's not enough to get a report that says, "Here's where we are and here's what we did." If financial reports act as a scorecard, you have to know how you're doing compared to what you anticipated while the game is in progress. It's too late after the game is over. In-progress reporting and measurement are the keys to alerting management of both large and small companies that corrective action may be necessary.

A prerequisite to meaningful in-progress reporting and measurement is a complete set of budgets. Any executive that attempts to manage his company without budgets is operating with one eye closed and one hand tied behind his back. Perhaps even worse, he's allowing his executives to operate that way too.

The Case Against Monthly P&L Reports

It may be sacrilegious to utter these words, but consider eliminating the monthly P&L statement. Why? Well, here are a few things to think about:

- How late after the end of the month do you get the P&L report for that month?
- How soon are you able to implement whatever corrective action is indicated by that P&L statement after you get it?
- Do you have to do a monthly physical inventory count as part of the preparation of the P&L?
- Do you have to estimate or use a theoretical "book" inventory figure to prepare the P&L?
- How many extra accounting people do you need to process the paperwork and data for the P&L report on schedule?

Monthly P&L reports are expensive to prepare and really may give you stale data, depending upon the sophistication of your accounting or computer system and the frenzy with which your accounting department works to prepare the statement. It may be worthwhile to skip the preparation of the monthly P&L and concentrate instead on such things as the "key data" report, certain specific "limited scope" reports, and the regular quarterly financial reports.

The Key Data Report

One of the easiest, most efficient ways to keep your finger on the pulse of the business is to create your own "key data" report. Just as there are certain vital readings that a physician will make to monitor the general health of a patient, so too are there vital bits of information that management can monitor regarding the company's health vis-à-vis the strategic plan. Ideally, the key data report (prepared not less than weekly) for the previous week should be on your desk and your senior managers' desks when you return from lunch each Monday. The contents of this report may vary among different company types, but the essence of your business—the important data that keeps you abreast of the status of your business—should be on that report.

The key data report is *not* prepared by accounting, although that department may provide some of the data. The secretary to the president or general manager should collect, prepare, and distribute the key data report based on specific information reported by other departments. Having the key data reportable to the top executive in headquarters emphasizes to all reporting areas the importance of accurate and timely data.

Key Data Components

Regardless of the type of business, some key data components will be common among most companies. Some data can be supplied by product line, territory, or any other meaningful breakdown. These include:

1. Net shipment dollars invoiced (sales) last week
2. Cumulative net shipment dollars invoiced (sales), month, quarter, and/or year-to-date
3. Order dollars booked last week
4. Cumulative order dollars booked, month, quarter, and/or year-to-date
5. Backlog dollars as of end of last week
6. Cash balance
7. Accounts receivable collected last week
8. Cash disbursed last week
9. Accounts-receivable balance at end of week
10. Number of employees, by department, including net change from the previous week

The key data information and report should be compared or correlated to the expected actual status per the budget and strategic plan at that point. Also, some of the key data information lends itself to charts or graphs as well as to some sort of comparison to a similar, prior period.

The information is or should be readily and routinely available from the appropriate departments without any hassle or without significantly involving the accounting department. For example,

- The weekly sales figures? Take an adding machine tape of the invoices and credit memos typed up and mailed last week by the billing department.
- Orders booked last week? Take an adding machine tape of all orders accepted by the sales department last week.
- Cash collections? Take an adding machine tape of the bank deposits made by the treasurer's office.
- Cash disbursements? Take an adding machine tape of all checks signed last week.
- Number of employees and net hires? Collect data from the personnel and/or payroll departments.
- Accounts receivable balance? Take last week's balance plus and minus the amounts reported as billed and collected this week.

The numbers don't have to be completely accurate. Dollar amounts can be rounded to the nearest thousand or ten thousand. Insignificant errors can be corrected in a subsequent week's numbers. If the error is significant and may distort the report, include an appropriate correction and explanation in the next report. Remember, the key data report is a "flash" report. It may sacrifice accounting-grade accuracy for speed, but it is invaluable for checking the business' status, progress against your strategic business plan, and as an early warning system.

Other Flash or Limited-Scope Reports and Data

In addition to the key data report, you can obtain early indications of potential problems weekly from the normal office or factory paperwork system. Every major department may have one or more expense categories or other points of measurement, the level of which may be symptomatic of their being on, ahead, or behind target. For example, on a weekly basis:

- The payroll department can provide the amount of overtime hours or rework hours in the factory.
- The purchasing department can provide the aggregate value of purchase orders issued, by major category—raw material or inventory purchases, repair and maintenance expense, capital equipment, etc.
- The company's travel agent can report the total cost of all airplane tickets ordered by company personnel.

- The switchboard operator can keep a weekly log of incoming calls from potential customers.
- The mixing department can provide the percentage of waste or spoilage, or the inspection department can indicate the number of dozens rejected, or the freezing department can report the number of pounds of meats processed.

Weeks, if not months, before the accounting department issues a formal P&L report, you should know what those results will be within reasonable limits. The reality is that only a handful of expense categories or revenue sources will vary significantly enough to have a major impact on the P&L or business plan. If you set up a flash report to monitor those items, you will keep yourself informed and the rest of the organization on its toes.

Responsibility Reporting

An essential concept in any useful management information system is "responsibility reporting"—that information must be provided to those who can do something about the problems disclosed. Just as management authority and responsibility must be correlated, information and reports have to be integrated as well. In general, as information flows up the company's organizational structure, data tend to become truncated, and important facts and figures may get obscured as they reach the senior levels. Accordingly, the design of the reports plus the "when, how, and to whom" the reports are transmitted must not be left to chance. Equally important in today's copy-happy society, you don't want everyone to be inundated with useless memos and reports.

Sideways Counts Too

It isn't always enough for important data to flow up the chain of command. Specific useful information must be distributed on the horizontal axis—across the peer level. Performance or status data from one department often have an immediate, crucial impact on the activities of other departments at the same organizational level. If the information has to flow up and then back downhill, you lose valuable time.

Chapter 11

Employees Are People Too

AMERICAN business managers have bemoaned the performance of the American worker for years, while at the same time installing human resource management programs, sophisticated motivation systems, and psychological testing procedures in an attempt to modify employee behavior. Once, craftsmanship, skills, hard work, and loyalty from the average factory or office employee was the accepted norm. Somewhere along the line, this was apparently lost, but by whom—by the employee or by management? Today, a fair share of many a company's budget is spent trying to adopt the concepts and findings of the behavioral science experts into their corporate culture—quality of work life (QWL), employee participation, quality circles—the gamut of today's human resource buzzwords and fads.

The View from the Top

Why is it that management needs so much outside help in achieving a working environment conducive to both employee productivity and satisfaction? Why does treating an employee with dignity and respect have to become a written policy, procedure, or a special project instead of a natural component of the management/employee relationship?

The growth in the labor union movement over the past few generations epitomizes the widening chasm between management and employee—and it's one charged with emotion and antagonism. This atmosphere is almost innate, existing even if an employee has never been a union member or a manager has never worked in a union environment. Regardless of the real or supposed merits of either party's position or arguments in any particular situation, management and worker bring a legacy of suspicion and hostility to almost every contact they have with one another.

Perhaps another reason can be found in the development of management as the kind of career path in which many of the travelers rarely have had hands-on experience in the work areas they will supervise. Their understanding of the real factory or office environment in which their subordinates work is sketchy at best. They have never spent time where the "rubber meets the road" and are unable to view matters from that perspective. Now that doesn't mean that all management personnel must work themselves up from the ranks, but it does mean that management must somehow acquire a strong sense of empathy for what things are like from the workers' viewpoint.

Finally, until recently members of a management team almost always conducted themselves as if they and they alone knew best in all matters; that the employee had little to offer except a strong back and skilled hands. Obviously, such a callous, uncaring attitude will be met with hostility and resentment.

It's Human Nature

You must have some understanding of human nature if you want to motivate your employees. The basic premise is that people tend to act in their own interests, with interests being defined as the satisfaction of their personal needs. One theory of human needs (the hierarchy-of-needs theory) postulates that people are motivated by five distinct types of needs, in the following order: physiological (food, clothing, shelter); safety (protection from danger); love (maintaining satisfying or affectionate relations with others); self-esteem (recognition, respect, and ego-stroking); self-fulfillment (achieving an individual's full potential for accomplishment and self-satisfaction).

It is easy to see how an individual's personal needs are operative in the company environment—wages sufficient to satisfy the physiological needs of the employee (as perceived by the employee), and safety in the workplace. These two needs are fundamental, and until they are met, an individual will be less driven by secondary needs, such as satisfactory relationships with co-workers and supervisors; recognition and reward for one's efforts, abilities, accomplishments, and skills; and upward mobility and potential.

The key task for management is to:

1. Structure the environment so the employee realizes, consciously or unconsciously, that the way to achieve satisfaction of those secondary needs is through work.
2. Provide and maintain an environment that will allow the satisfaction of those secondary needs.

A Piece or a Person?

Major difficulties begin when a company treats employees as "pieces" rather than as thinking and feeling people. Whether the individuals are executives or regular employees, you will create a negative reputation for yourself and damage your company's image as a fair and desirable place to work and seek a career. It won't be too long before morale, efficiency, and productivity begin to decline. In response to that decline, the typical company then brings in the experts and installs a battery of remedial programs in a superficial effort to improve the "corporate culture." Unfortunately, many of these shallow programs are really manipulative schemes designed to lull the employees into a more malleable mass. The basic company-employee problems remain, only they are covered with a veneer of approaches that haven't changed a thing.

The moral to be learned is that people are not easily deceived for very long. It is true you can modify the behavior of people through scientific techniques, but positive long-term results depend upon a company environment that respects the dignity, intelligence, and physical and emotional well-being of its employees.

What is it that employees want? Job satisfaction is the euphemistic term generally applied, but what does that mean? A fair wage certainly, but perhaps more important, it means being treated with respect and dignity for the work they do, for the knowledge and talent they have to offer, and for the trust and commitment they give to the company. In short, they wish to be treated like human beings, not a very radical, earth-shaking proposition after all.

Loyalty and Pride: A Two-Way Street

How a person behaves in an organization is to a large degree dependent upon how that person views the nature of the organization itself. People are adaptive, and to satisfy their needs for dignity and self-esteem they will respond in ways designed to satisfy those needs regardless of the organization's environment or rules. In negative corporate environments, those responses sometimes seem irrational to management and not in the best interests of the employee or the company—perhaps destructive to the future welfare of both. "Don't they understand?" management asks itself; probably not, but then again, neither does management. In positive corporate environments, the picture is quite different. The employee responds with loyalty and pride, and in concert with what is beneficial to the company's welfare.

A company's environment or "culture" is a peculiar creation—simultaneously resilient and strong in the face of economic adversity but fragile and easily shattered by the actions of the company's executives.

*

Ranger Toy Company, a successful forty-year-old publicly owned company, produced childrens' toys and precision metal castings of collectible miniature historical figures. It enjoyed significant market share despite competition from cheaper, lower-quality imports. The nonunion company maintained a close relationship with its three hundred employees, many of whom possessed hard-to-replace skills for doing the delicate, final finishing handwork. A long history of employee loyalty existed; many employees were second-generation. Employees and executives were on a first-name basis, and the company atmosphere was friendly and informal while still businesslike and efficient. Traditionally, most promotions had been made from within.

Two years ago, the president of Ranger hired Mr. Robert Nave to be vice-president of engineering, a newly created position. When the president was suddenly killed in a plane crash, Mr. Nave became president by default after two senior executives declined for reasons of health. Intelligent and capable, Mr. Nave had not been comfortable with the conditions at Ranger. His ten years' experience as chief engineer at his previous employer, a unionized division of a large, impersonal multinational conglomerate, were at odds with Ranger's corporate environment.

When he became president, Mr. Nave assembled his own "team" to make the company "more businesslike." He asked for the resignations of the vice-presidents of sales and finance (the two officers who had refused the presidency), whom he viewed as relics of the past. New vice-presidents (none of whom had any experience in the toy business) were hired. Shortly thereafter, the general sales manager, the corporate controller, and the manufacturing manager were fired and replaced from outside the company, as were several other departmental supervisors. Mr. Nave did not promote from within the company, seeking instead to bring in people with new attitudes and whose loyalty would be to him personally.

Within eighteen months, Mr. Nave and his new team had gutted the company of experienced executives and skilled workers and stripped the company of its unique personality—a vital but intangible asset that had contributed to its success over the years. Ranger Toy lost its market share, its profitability, and the respect and loyalty of its employees. Without professional help, Mr. Nave and his team will be powerless to tackle the major rebuilding job ahead.

*

A Positive Corporate Environment: What Is It?

The health of the corporate environment starts at the top. The senior managers must believe that it's possible to operate a profit-making enterprise and still provide a good work place for all employees. Without that conviction and the actions required to turn that conviction into reality, little can be achieved.

Some of the unique characteristics of a positive corporate environment include:

1. The opportunity for advancement and upward mobility for everyone, with the chance to improve skills, wages, level of responsibility, and authority. This requires job descriptions, and fair performance appraisals, without favoritism, whose objectives are to improve employee performance and recognize and reward accomplishment.

2. The recognition that employees at every level can offer useful and valuable suggestions, input, and insights. Intelligence, knowledge, and skill are not the exclusive property of management personnel. Open, two-way lines of communication must exist between employee and supervisor to create a positive environment.

3. Employees should have a voice in and control over certain aspects of their total work environment. This translates into granting the employees some power, always somewhat of a threat to most managers. Yet, by attempting to keep the employees completely powerless, management runs an even greater long-range risk. Employees will seek power in other ways, perhaps in ways that will be detrimental to the company's interests.

A company is most certainly not a democracy, but allowing employees some power does not mean shifting to anarchy. What it does mean is granting some latitude and autonomy to employees and line supervisors. There is no meter or gauge to tell you how far to go. It is a process that should start slowly as the participants feel their way. Because the granting or sharing of certain powers is a top management prerogative, it can always, at some risk of repercussion, be tapered off or cut off if necessary. However, because the benefits the company can derive are so large, empowering those previously powerless can be an important step in creating a positive work environment.

Know Your People And Let Them Know You

When you remain remote and aloof from the people in your organization, you create a barrier in the path of a positive environment. No one expects you to completely be "one of the guys" either, but there is a large middle ground between the two extremes. One word of caution: If you really are a loner and unable to relate to others with sincerity and naturalness, then you shouldn't try this. You will only appear phony.

Do you ever just stroll through the factory and offices, stopping to say hello with an employee here and there (making sure you know their name), inquiring about their health, family, Sunday's football game—basically making small talk? If the company has a bowling league or softball team, do you and other executives participate? If you don't, do you show up to cheer, or with a dozen pizzas and soft drinks for the gang, sticking around to share it with them? Do you let everyone know that, despite your position of authority, you are a caring person? Of course the larger the company, the more difficult it is for executives to do this, but you should set the example and let everyone know that this conduct is the norm in your company. You can build up an enormous reservoir of goodwill, which will be a great asset in difficult times.

There are other things you can do to create a positive company environment. For example, you could install a free "employee assistance program" for the confidential use of employees facing personal or family crises. Relatively inexpensive, these programs can help in relieving personal pressures and worries from the shoulders of your employees.

Do you take the time to explain in advance major shifts or changes in corporate strategy or programs? Do so in person if possible, or use videotapes if timing and geography are a problem. Such a practice directly acknowledges the employees' right to know what is going on—a "quid pro quo" for their loyalty. At the least, send a personal letter or note to each employee. Make sure all supervisory levels receive an in-depth briefing beforehand so they can respond to the questions and concerns of the employees.

Quid Pro Quo

There is a practical reason for management concern regarding employee satisfaction: The survival of a company can depend upon it. It's fairly certain you will not be able to create the perfect working environment for all employees; there will always be a few malcontents in any organization. But if the majority of employees are responsive to management's new behavior, positive company environment, and honest concern regarding their welfare, your burdens as manager will be lightened. Employee efficiency and motivation will increase, absenteeism and lateness will decline, quality will go up, scrap and waste will go down. In short, almost every aspect of the company's operations will improve, and so will its present and future outlook. Not a bad return for being a good guy.

Chapter 12

Management by Objectives

OVER the last quarter century, in response to their search for more effective methods of directing and coordinating the diverse resources of their organizations, many chief executives have adopted a technique of management referred to as "management by objectives" (MBO). You might want to examine the benefits that installing an MBO system could offer your company, but be aware that an MBO may involve a complete reshaping of your company's management structure, starting with you.

A MIRACLE CURE?

At first glance, MBO has a seductive simplicity—a getting to the heart of the matter—that belies the true complexity and requirements of a successful MBO program. Almost everyone zeros in on the word "objectives" because pleasant visions of deadlines being met, projects being completed on time and within budget, or new markets penetrated dance in the eyes of the beholder—at last, a magic wand for management. In reality, the operative word in MBO is "management," not "objectives." Not recognizing this distinction up front almost always dooms the program to failure and the entire company to disappointment and frustration, no matter how well intentioned management was.

The reason is simple: What seems like the ruthless efficiency of the MBO approach to business management evokes an overwhelming temptation to implement the plan without understanding its complexities and environmental preconditions. Those who rush in blindly react in a typical manner: A senior manager calls in a key subordinate, asks the subordinate to write down a few worthy-sounding objectives to be accomplished during the next "rating" period, shakes hands, and wishes him luck. He then goes through the same process with the next subordinate. Such an approach is not MBO.

Magnetic North: Setting the Basic Objective

Pick up a recent annual report of almost any public corporation and somewhere, probably on the inside front cover, will be a "mission statement"—a set of corporate objectives expressed in broadly worded phrases whose attainment would gladden the heart of any shareholder. In the ideal business world, all decisions and efforts of the directors, officers, and employees of the company are supposed to be made in the context of that mission statement.

Someone once referred to the corporate mission statement as the compass that keeps the company and its personnel on track. A more accurate description is that the mission statement is the magnetic pole from which the compass directions are charted, because a company must often make or suffer some deviations from the planned course without losing track of its goals and objectives. Unfortunately, corporate mission statements may be so broadly worded that they are useful only as general guidelines. Thus, well-defined corporate objectives are a necessary precondition before attempting to implement a useful MBO system.

Starting at the Top

A plan to use MBO in an organization must start at the top, with corporate objectives. Assuming—and this is critical—that the objectives established by the highest executive level are in accordance with one another, then each subordinate level of management and other personnel must develop their objectives in the context of the expressed goals of the higher and peer levels. Thus, the objectives of each level overlap with those of adjacent levels, both horizontally and vertically, and must therefore be in support of, or supported by, the adjacent levels' objectives. With such consonance of action and unity of thought in its component parts, the company as a whole can be stronger and more efficient. However, if each level of the company sets its own objectives and priorities with no thought to the unity displayed at the higher levels, intracompany and interdepartmental integration cannot be achieved. The resulting chaos would destroy the company from within.

Because objectives must be integrated in the typical multilevel or multidepartment organization, MBO cannot be viewed as a quick-fix or one-shot operation. You need a complete "systems approach" when you implement an MBO program. A companywide educational program covering the concept, implementation, and proper use of an MBO program is the first place to begin.

Communication, Prioritization, and Coordination

While it may seem that the company's goals should initially flow from the board of directors down to the lower echelons, it is usually more realistic to have the senior executives, line and staff (as a working committee under the president), formulate a set of specific objectives to be submitted to the board of directors. The board, working with the president, then reviews the recommendations and agrees upon a balanced, realistic, coordinated set of goals. The president then communicates those goals to the senior executive group for followup and implementation.

With the overall corporate objectives delineated, the members of the senior executive group, probably at the vice-presidential level, develop objectives for their own areas. Critical at this point is the need for good communications among departments—finance, sales, manufacturing, engineering, personnel—so that each supports the others' objectives. Working out the objectives for their various areas enables the vice-presidents to agree on priorities, allocate resources, and provide support to one another. Regardless of the department, its objectives must conform with the overall corporate goals.

The vice-presidents then meet with their next immediate subordinate level to outline the corporate objectives and develop a set of recommendations. The subordinate is responsible for developing a set of objectives for his or her sphere of responsibility, which, in turn, will support the higher-level objectives. The same process flows down the organizational chain through every subordinate level and department.

While the flow of objectives is from the "top down," an MBO system is not a series of direct orders flowing down the chain of command. The specific objectives for each level are not set by the next highest level—only the context within which those objectives must be formulated is established.

Not all objectives have to relate specifically to the corporate objectives or those of an adjacent area. A manager can establish supplementary objectives that relate solely to activities within that manager's area or are personal goals of the manager.

Getting from Here to There

Setting objectives is only part of the task of implementing an MBO system. Managers must have a realistic plan for accomplishing their objectives. No matter how admirable the goal and enthusiastically it is agreed upon, if it cannot be accomplished or there is no logical plan for its accomplishment, the objective is worthless. Before a manager agrees to accept a subordinate's objectives, the subordinate must provide a realistic plan detailing how and when each objective will be realized. Objectives that amount to nothing more than wishful thinking or impractical pipe dreams must be rejected.

Allowing Time for Results

The "what" of the objective must be matched with a "when." Objectives cannot be open-ended; they must contain a time element, a specific date by which each objective will be accomplished. A few objectives may have a relatively short-term target date, say three to six months; others may require a year or more. Regardless of the time allowed to meet an objective, don't pressure managers for near-term results and thus jeopardize real, long-term accomplishments.

Mid-Course Corrections

There should be periodic reviews to revalidate or fine-tune the objectives, reinvigorate the process, and recognize and/or reward for progress made to date. Regular reviews can also provide managers with time to take corrective action before the target date. In general, reviews should take place every three months.

Ownership of Objectives

Because managers at each level set their own objectives (although in the context of the higher level's objectives), they may assume personal ownership and direct responsibility for the successful achievement of those objectives. When a manager makes a commitment to accomplish those objectives, he or she provides a motivation that is difficult to duplicate. In a well-structured MBO system, a manager should derive personal benefit—promotions, bonuses, larger salary increases—when the objectives he or she established are met.

Administering the MBO System

While the MBO system applies to all areas of the company, one individual should be assigned responsibility for its administration. The paperwork, record-keeping, and coordination details associated with the system could be delegated to the chief financial officer, as it is in many companies, or to any senior officer. The administrator will consolidate all objectives from each corporate level, create a calendar of "status-check" dates specifying the target dates (as set forth in the objectives themselves), and prepare interim reports, which will allow top management to control and evaluate results. The administrator also checks the objectives for obvious conflicts or for any that may be at cross-purposes. Note that *administrator* of the MBO system does not mean *manager* of the system. The system is under the authority of the president of the company, who uses it as a management technique.

All objectives from every level must be clearly stated in writing with a target completion date. A copy should be forwarded to the MBO administrator for review and compilation. Managers at each level should retain copies of immediate subordinates' objectives. In some cases, the manager may choose to receive a copy of the objectives of all subordinate managers two levels down in order to monitor how the immediate subordinate is dealing with his or her supervisory responsibilities.

In general, depending on company size, the president usually monitors only the objectives of the senior line and staff officers reporting to him. Below the vice-presidential or senior-officer level, objectives need not be distributed *across* subdepartmental lines.

Objectives that are completely dependent upon the cooperation and coordination of two or more separately managed departments should be avoided, especially below the vice-presidential level. A key element of the MBO system may be weakened by co-ownership. For example, two managers may assign the same objective different priorities, different resources, perhaps even a different interpretation. It is better to break the objective down into component parts for each area to accept and deal with on their own.

While the administrator of the MBO system performs certain recording and collating functions, the individual managers will followup on the progress made toward attaining the objectives set by their subordinates. This should be a one-on-one process, with the manager dealing directly with each next-subordinate manager in that area.

Judging the Results

Using an MBO system effectively will yield many positive results besides the obvious one of attaining specified objectives. You can expect managers to become more goal-oriented and motivated in addition to their becoming better planners and supervisors. The entire performance evaluation system in the company will get better, with positive results upon the administration of the always troublesome employee compensation plan. Many of the internal systems of the company—budgeting, financial reporting, policies, procedures—will change for the better.

You and the company should be prepared for another, perhaps traumatic surprise. Implementing an MBO system sometimes reveals the incompetence or the failure of some managers and employees to measure up to the new standards of performance, and you may be disturbed at who they are. What you do with that realization is up to you, but a failure to address the issue squarely may have serious side effects.

You should not expect an MBO system to be implemented without some problems, resistance, or confusion. Having someone on your staff who has had experience or training in an MBO environment would be a great help in doing the necessary training, explaining, and debugging.

Given enough time and cooperation, in a year or two, your company can establish a well-functioning, productive MBO system that assists you by forging an integrated chain of corporate and employee objectives, all directed to improving growth, profitability, financial stability, and employee welfare.

PART 3

Keeping Score

REGARDLESS of a company president's background, the position requires that he or she be a generalist and learn to deal with a wide range of operational issues. Included among these are financial, sales, marketing, and quality considerations. Many companies have specialists on the management team for those areas, yet that does not relieve the company president or general manager from the awesome responsibility of having ultimate accountability. It is vital that the person in charge make it his or her business to learn and understand more of the day-to-day nitty-gritty business operations that affect the bottom line.

Chapter 13

Cash, The Staff of Business Life

TWO men were discussing the recent death of one of their mutual acquaintances. "What did he die of?" one of them asked. "A lack of life," was the oversimplified but accurate response. If the question had been about the death of a business, another oversimplified, but probably accurate, response would have been, "a lack of cash."

Cash and cash flow are the lifeblood of any business. Given that no business has an unlimited source of funds, it follows that the continued existence of every business is dependent upon the relationship of the speed and volume of cash flowing from the business to the speed and volume of cash coming into the business.

If we eliminate all the confusing accounting distractions, high-tech mumbo-jumbo, and marketing machinations, the fundamental operation of any business is to convert its cash into marketable merchandise or a service product, sell that product, and receive payment of a larger amount of cash, completing that cycle in as short a period of time as possible. So the factors we are concerned with are "How much?" and "How fast?"

Understanding the Cash Flow Cycle

It is the rare business that generates surplus cash quickly. Some service businesses that require little or no inventory are able to generate immediate cash sales, but most businesses require an investment in inventory, receivables from customers, and perhaps some equipment, tools, or machinery. The average business has three major "holes" into which cash is "sunk"—inventory, capital assets, and accounts receivable. These are not permanent "sinkholes," for the cash does circulate out of those holes, usually on a reasonably predictable time basis. This "circulation" of cash over a period of time is the "cash flow cycle."

Obviously, the quicker the circulation, the less overall cash investment will be required to sustain the business. The velocity of cash flow can vary significantly from business to business, depending on many circumstances, but that rate is often highly dependent upon the policies adopted by management and the diligence with which management does its job. An absence of inventory planning, overbuying of merchandise, or bad stockroom management can tie up large amounts of cash unnecessarily. A too-liberal credit policy or poor followup on past-due accounts receivable can be disastrous to your cash flow.

Profit Is Not Cash and Vice Versa

An important step to securing your company's continued survival is to learn the difference between accrual-basis accounting, cash-basis accounting, and cash flow. Accrual-basis and cash-basis are record-keeping techniques, whereas "cash flow" is the business cycle through which the company uses its cash to generate profit and increase equity.

A surprising number of business managers and executives have trouble reconciling their company's favorable P&L statement (usually prepared on an accrual basis) with its chronic, but normal, shortage of cash. "If we made a hundred thousand in profit last year," one manager asks, "why can't we pay our vendors on time?"

Simply stated, a cash-basis financial report ignores all amounts owed *to* the company (usually customer accounts receivable) and the sales revenue derived from such uncollected accounts. It also ignores all amounts owed *by* the company (usually accounts payable) and the expenses, inventory, and equipment by which those payables were created. Because a cash-basis report omits an enormous amount of the company's financial activities, it is a distorted picture of its performance. Few companies today use cash-basis accounting in preparing financial reports, but executives not trained in accounting may find it difficult to think in terms other than "cash-basis."

Stretching Your Cash

Managers make use of many programs to reduce their cash expenditures and increase cash income, including planning, budgeting, inventory control, expense monitoring, receivables and credit management, and other important macro-approaches. Many excellent books are available describing such sound business procedures, most of which you should already be using. However, cash can also be conserved in micro-bites, using somewhat unorthodox methods that might not be "cricket," but you might want to give them a try. If you don't try them, you'll never know.

Nibbling at the Outflow

The larger your bank balance, the better the chances of your business surviving, and the more time, management options, and flexibility you have to meet unexpected situations. An important source of the necessary cash to operate a business is the amount of open credit (via your accounts payable) you receive from your suppliers, the length of time before you have to pay those vendor invoices, and how much you finally pay. Anything you can do to reduce the speed or cut down the volume of the outflow enhances the survivability (and probably the profitability) of your business.

You should exempt your small, thinly capitalized suppliers and contractors from these tactics, especially if you are an important segment of their business volume. Their continued survival may depend upon your prompt, timely payment.

Rule 1: Always try to pay your bills moderately late.

What's that you said? That's sacrilege—you'll ruin your credit rating. Nonsense, almost everyone else is doing it, so why not you? The operative words are "moderately late." Take a look at your own customer base. Do your biggest and best customers pay all of your invoices exactly when they are due? And if they don't, are you prepared to stop shipping to them? Probably not; you take their check that is ten or twenty days late and you deposit it, thankful it wasn't even later, and keep on shipping.

The days of businesses paying their bills on a regular net 30-day basis are long gone. Large and small businesses now accept that most of their receivables will be collected in sixty days, some thirty days after the usually typical net 30-day terms originally agreed upon.

When trying to collect from a company that is otherwise perfectly capable of paying on time, you may get a variety of responses from the accounts-payable department, from stonewalling to the old chestnut

"The check is in the mail." Or you may get more sophisticated responses:

> "We know your invoice was due on the fifth, but our computer system only prepares disbursement checks on the third Thursday of the month," or some similar response that places the blame on the infamous, inflexible computer system.

> "We measure the 30-day period from the time the merchandise is actually received by us," or "passes our incoming quality control," or "is signed off by our purchasing department," or some other unalterable internal procedure to which your invoice is subject.

The lesson to be learned is, if it works for them, why not for you? You too should prepare your disbursement checks as few times a month as possible—twice a month if necessary, once a month if possible. The reality is, you don't have to be consistent among your various suppliers. With some, you can get away with it; with others, you may run into problems and have to make exceptions. Only by trying will you determine the limits to which you can go without adversely affecting your relationship with that supplier.

Rule 2: Never mail your disbursement checks before Friday afternoon.

It is relatively easy to make the U.S. Postal Service the scapegoat for some of your cash conservation practices, while your company derives the benefits. You can also pick up a few days' grace for taking discounts and meeting net due dates. Consider the following setup in your company:

1. You have a standard postage meter machine in your company that places a dated postage impression on the envelope.
2. You prepare your disbursement checks on the second and fourth Thursdays of each month, and the checks are so dated.
3. The checks are inserted in envelopes and run through the postage meter so that the meter impresses Thursday's date on the envelope.
4. The envelopes with the checks are not actually mailed by you

until Friday afternoon, so that your vendors do not receive your payments until the following Monday at the earliest.

The effect of this subterfuge is to retain the cash in your own accounts for the maximum length of time, while the paper trail (check date and envelope date) supports a payment history of being made at an earlier date. It is true that the vendor doesn't receive the check until at least four days (Friday through Monday) from the date on the check, but in today's universal condemnation of the Postal Service, such delays are commonplace and rarely disputed. The vendor's accounts-receivable personnel will probably not question your dating. If they do, blame the Postal Service and keep doing it.

Rule 3: Never mail your disbursement checks to a lock-box address; send them to the company's actual street address.

Many companies specify a lock-box address on their invoices to which you are supposed to send your payment. This address is usually that of the vendor's bank, so arranged in order to collect the funds transmitted by the check drawn on your bank to their bank account more quickly. Sending the check to the company's main office and not the lock-box can keep the money in your bank account (earning interest) for one to three more days. Frequently, companies relying upon a lock-box setup are not efficient in processing and depositing checks that are received directly at their offices. They may sit around a few days before enough checks are accumulated to make it "worthwhile" to send a clerk over to the bank with a deposit.

Rule 4: Never wait to get a vendor's credit memo; always issue your own debit memo in the amount you believe is correct, and deduct it when making your next payment. Alternatively, withhold payment on any invoice (make no partial payments) on which you have a valid dispute until the dispute is corrected via a credit memo or other adjustment.

In applying this rule, it is important to promptly notify your vendor of the item(s) in question so that you can retain the "moral high ground." Obviously, the claim should be a valid and defensible one.

Rule 5: Calculate the true net benefit before you decide to take the cash discounts offered by your suppliers for accelerated payment of any invoice.

Your decision to take a cash discount should depend on what interest rate you can earn on your idle cash, or what interest rate you are paying if you are a borrower, measured against the discount rate offered by the supplier. Concurrent with that calculation, you should stretch the time allowed for taking a cash discount for accelerated payment for as long as you can get away with.

For example, assume a vendor offers a ½ percent cash discount on a $1,000.00 invoice dated March 1, if it is paid within 10 days—by March 11; full payment is due in 30 days, on April 1. You can earn interest at a 6 percent annual rate on your money if you invest it with your bank. Should you take the discount? For the sake of simplicity, we will ignore "float" and "in-transit" time, although once you understand the decision-making process, such times should be included in your calculation:

> $1,000 less ½ percent discount = a $5 saving if $995 is paid 20 days before it is actually due.

> Alternatively, that same $995 invested for 20 days at a 6 percent annual interest rate = $995 × 6 percent × 20 days/365 days = $3.27, which can be earned if you don't take the discount.

In this case, you would take the discount, assuming you had the funds available.

Suppose, however, you are using bank debt as the source of your cash, and that debt incurred bank interest at a 12 percent annual rate. Borrowing $995 on March 11, some 20 days in advance of when it would otherwise be necessary (on April 11), would cost you $6.54 ($995 × 12 percent × 20 days/365 days). You probably should not take the discount.

If, using one of these delay subterfuges, you were able to stretch the discount period to 16 days, then the cost to borrow the $995 would drop to $4.58 ($995 × 12 percent × 14 days/365 days), and your decision might be different.

If a vendor who has received your check on which there was a "late" discount taken calls to protest, you should apologize, tell them to return the uncashed check, and say that you will pay the full invoice amount in another two weeks when the invoice is due. You will probably find that nine out of ten vendors will allow the discount rather than return the check.

Rule 6: Don't pay your employees on a weekly basis.

Every two weeks is better; once a month is best. Many companies pay their employees a week behind; that is, the paycheck disbursed on, say, March 14 is for the workweek ending on March 7. This effectively gives the company a permanent investment of one week's worth of labor from each employee. Obviously, if you have a policy of paying every two weeks or once a month, you are that much further ahead of the game. You will have more cash in your company's bank accounts earning interest or meeting average or compensating balance requirements. Even if you can't do it across the board for both hourly and salaried personnel, you might be able to adopt that schedule for the salaried personnel.

Harvesting the Inflow

Obviously, you can improve your cash position by taking certain steps to speed up your billing process and the collection of all your receivables. Surprisingly and unfortunately, most businesses do not give enough attention to the billing and collection processes. This management failure is usually evidenced by having underqualified, underpaid individuals in charge of the billing and collection/credit management function. In addition, senior nonaccounting management personnel rarely, if ever, review the detailed accounts-receivable trial balance. The only time a company officer, other than the chief accounting officer, sees the status and the details of the company's receivables is when one or more of the accounts is seriously past due.

Rule 1: The chief financial officer should review receivables at least twice a month and preferably weekly. All other officers should review the details of all the accounts receivable at least monthly, preferably more often.

Rule 2: Keep the sales force (outside and inside, independent or captive) apprised of actual or potential receivable problems with various customer accounts.

If, for some reason, you do not engage the sales force in the collection process, you should certainly make sure they are part of the communication process. For example, they should know the right people at the customer's facility to whom copies of past-due invoices should be delivered and from whom explanations of problems or comments should be obtained.

Rule 3: Shorten the time interval between the date of the shipment of your product (or service) and the date the invoice for that shipment is mailed to the customer by your billing department.

It is not uncommon to find, on a regular and routine basis, that invoices are not being mailed to customers until days, perhaps weeks, after the merchandise has actually been dispatched to the customer. Even though the invoice may be dated with the same date as the shipment, the internal billing system (or lack thereof) takes so much time that days may pass as the paperwork grinds its way through the organization. The customer, on the other hand, will not expedite payment for an invoice that is received late.

Rule 4: Make certain the description of the material on your invoice matches or includes the description used by the customer in his purchase order.

Many large companies issuing purchase orders use their own terminology and descriptions to specify what they are ordering. These descriptions can differ significantly from the way you routinely describe those same products on your invoice and packing slips. For example, you may describe one of your product shipments as:

Quantity 12 YourCompany Inc. Model A10 motorized, digital, LED read-out, super-accurate weighing balances @ $99.00 ea

The customer describes the very same merchandise in his purchase order as:

Quantity 1 Dozen Electronic Scales—$1,188.00

Your people know what they want and ship the correct merchandise promptly. However, until the personnel at the customer's receiving, purchasing, and accounts-payable departments are able to match up the necessary documents to permit payment, your invoice will languish in the "I'm too lazy to work out this confusion" pile that every accounts-payable clerk has in one of the desk drawers.

Bow to reality and make certain that your company provides the supplemental information—copies of the customer's purchase order with both your packing slip and invoice when they are sent to the customer. Make it as easy as possible for all documentation to fit the customer's idiosyncrasies.

Rule 5: As a general rule, don't offer a cash discount for "prompt" payment.

Prompt-payment discounts usually cost you more than they are worth, and your customers will usually abuse the conditions for earning the discount. Also, once started, a cash-discount policy is difficult to discontinue. A cash discount is an appropriate tactic to bring in some cash quicker, however, if you have no more bank credit available, or if you must fight competitive factors.

Rule 6: Never send out a monthly statement of accounts receivable to a customer if that statement shows that you owe your customer money or he has credit memos in his favor.

You would be surprised how often a credit memo will be overlooked for weeks or months. Besides, customers are always unilaterally taking their own debit memos against payments made to you for one thing or another that are never explained and rarely justified.

In general, statements are a waste of effort and postage; they usually end up in the wastebasket at the customer's accounts-payable department. If a statement was to get a reaction, the customer would probably only request details on the past-due items anyway. It's far better to send the customer a copy of the invoice (plus supporting shipping data and purchase order copy) that is past due with an appropriate note directing attention to the invoice.

Rule 7: The billing supervisor and credit manager are vital to a company's cash flow. Make certain those persons are aggressive in fulfilling their responsibilities. In return, they should be compensated fairly and recognized for their contributions.

The last thing you want in those positions are individuals who follow a static policy of "Well, that's the way we always do it. We can't change things. Our customers won't allow it."

Rule 8: Use a lock-box for collections, if appropriate.

In any case, never permit customers' checks to sit around undeposited because someone is too busy or too lazy to drive to the bank. If your mail is delivered in the afternoon, make arrangements to have all your mail held at the post office for your pickup in the morning by your own personnel. Open mail and process checks immediately. There is no reason why a check received in the morning cannot be deposited in your bank account before 3 P.M. that afternoon.

Rule 9: Do not permit any of your customers to perpetrate the tactics on your company described in "Nibbling at the Outflow."

THE LIFEBLOOD OF THE COMPANY

Cash is a most precious and versatile commodity. It can buy you time, talent, and the ability to outlast a number of crises. Cash is difficult and expensive to obtain and hard to retain. When you are in business, you are in a constant battle for survival. As the leader of your company, you are fully justified in adopting methods, procedures, and tactics that will give you an advantage over your competition.

Chapter 14
Banks and Borrowing

ASK any banker about borrowing from his bank and he will be quick to tell you that "banks are in the business of lending money." What he doesn't say is:

- They want to be repaid in full and on time—no *ifs*, *ands*, or *buts*.
- They want to earn interest and other income from their relationship with you.
- The career progress of the banking officer depends upon his being able to generate loan volume and other service revenue for the bank that is profitable, trouble-free, and repetitive.

There is nothing wrong with a bank looking out for its interests first. That's how it should be. What is wrong is allowing yourself to be lulled into a false sense of security during the more halcyon days of your relationship with the bank. You must expect the bank to play hardball with you if your company is not in the best financial shape and your future is vulnerable. You may be invited to the annual golf outing of the bank, be sent box-seat tickets to a baseball game, receive a paperweight at Christmastime, but, at the core, bankers are lenders of money at a profit and expect to be paid in full as promised. Nothing more and nothing less.

"We're Here to Help You"

At the center of your relationship with the bank is the "account or loan officer." He is your advocate and adversary, adviser and disciplinarian, giver and collector, all rolled up in one. However, beyond that one man or woman stands a hierarchy and a bureaucracy loaded with rules and regulations. As pleasant and cooperative as the "account officer" may be, that person is only the tip of the iceberg.

Establish your personal relationship with the account officer of the bank as early as possible, even if you have no immediate plans or intentions to borrow. Interact with the account officer regularly: meet for lunch; give plant visits; submit financial data; take out a small loan or two and pay it back; use their cash management and/or lock-box system; buy a few of their certificates of deposit. By doing so, you won't be a stranger when you need to do some serious borrowing.

Just a Small Loan to Tide Us Over

The reason for borrowing must make good business sense. When you think about borrowing, you must also consider how you will meet the downstream payment demands of the interest costs and principal repayments. Ask yourself whether the loan will directly enhance your company's ability to improve its profits within the same time-frame as the loan repayment?

One of the classic problems many businesses create for themselves is using short-term debt to finance activities that should be funded through long-term financing or additional equity capital. A company that has seasonal peaks in work-in-process, finished goods, or accounts receivable and needs limited-period financing to handle such demands can readily use short-term borrowing, then repay those loans when the peak has passed, receivables are being collected, and the cash flow turns positive. But to use short-term demand debt as the primary means to finance a continuing, increasing need for working capital is usually a dangerous strategy.

In general, growing companies are consumers of working capital—more and more funds are tied up in inventory and receivables as the sales volume increases. The manufacturing cycle and collection time to convert today's incoming customer order into a cash collection can be six to twelve months or more. As each month goes by, with more and more orders coming in, the demands for additional cash will multiply. Business is good; it's growing, but so is the amount of the short-term demand debt.

YOU'VE BEEN A GOOD ACCOUNT, BUT . . .

Banks love to finance growing, profitable companies with a variety of secured, short-term loan packages. In fact, it's sometimes almost so easy to obtain a loan that many business managers fail to recognize that their larger company needs more permanent capital, either in the form of equity or long-term debt. In this case, long-term debt is defined as payable in five or more years. Before you sign up for a short-term loan, carefully consider the flip side of the equation—the "what-if?" Short-term debt can set you up for some nasty, unexpected surprises:

1. Sales growth could falter, leaving you with the momentum of your manufacturing and inventory buildup and their continuing drain on cash resources. In a relatively short time, you are no longer generating enough cash to meet your interest payments and are setup for a call of the loan or a cut-off of your line of credit.

2. You could experience a marked deterioration of gross margins and net profits because of competitor's price-cutting or manufacturing problems. This could adversely affect the vital differential between costs and revenues and prevent you from qualifying for and repaying your loans. You have little, if any, time to ride out and solve the business problem.

3. Given that most short-term loans have interest rates tied to a fluctuating prime rate, your cost of borrowed funds may exceed your margins of profit.

4. Your bank may unilaterally have a change of policy or personnel that will alter its relationship with your company, even though it has nothing to do with you. The bank may refuse to expand your credit line, may change the formula for computing loan limits, may want "out" of your industry, or any number of other things that could disrupt your company's plans for meeting its major cash requirements.

5. Other capital markets upon which you were depending to replace the short-term debt may be unavailable to you. You may have planned to raise new equity by publicly offering stock, or you may expect to negotiate a long-term loan with an insurance company or other financial institution. Those capital markets from time to time are not receptive or available to you. If your company has been overly dependent on short-term debt and has no flexibility or reserve borrowing power when other capital markets are closed, you will be put under enormous pressure by the very bank that seemed so cooperative earlier.

That pressure could force you to alter your strategic plans and take steps in the near-term that could impair your longer-term potential and opportunities.

The lesson to be learned is that a company's ability to obtain and take down short-term debt is a useful tool for management to employ. However, it is not a permanent foundation upon which to base the company's financial structure. Recognize it for what it is: a temporary prop that eventually should be replaced by appropriate additional capital.

Fine Print Means Big Hurdles

Whether borrowing short-term or long-term, never agree to a repayment schedule or other terms that depend on the perfect and timely execution of all of your company's business plans and expectations. Allow yourself some slack. Nothing ever works out exactly as planned, and if you don't retain some flexibility (in time, money, or freedom of action), you will most surely live to regret it.

Short- and long-term loan agreements are usually loaded with specific do's, cannot's, must meet's, and agree to's. You must be sure you understand the present and future implications and dangers that exist in the various terms, conditions, and covenants.

If you must give collateral, try to avoid giving a general filing or security lien on all your assets. Give only the collateral related to the specific loan. Thus, if a bank is granting you a loan pegged to your total accounts receivable, then pledge only the receivables; don't, for example, give them a lien against your equipment, machinery, or patents too.

Loan agreements often contain covenants that require the company's balance sheet and income statement to continue to meet certain criteria, such as:

- A current ratio of not less than a specific minimum
- Working capital of not less than a specific amount
- Net worth of not less than a specific amount
- A debt-to-equity ratio (total debt/total equity) of not more than a specific maximum
- A debt coverage ratio (profit before interest and taxes/annual principal and interest on debt) of not less than a specific minimum

The criteria tests may have to be met continuously or at specific times (monthly, quarterly, annually), as reflected on the company's financial statements.

Unfortunately, it is easy to trip over one or more of these covenants and be in technical default of the loan. Technical default can result in the bank calling the loan, changing the loan terms, raising the interest rate, or otherwise making life difficult for the company.

Covenants are *not* to be taken lightly. The president, the chief financial officer, and the board of directors of the company must, as part of the preborrowing analysis and projections, recognize the restrictions, limitations, and dangers posed by the covenants on future management decisions. After receiving a loan with covenants, management must ensure that current decisions or newly anticipated business conditions will not result in a future breach of a covenant.

If you and management suspect that a breach might occur, talk to the lending institution as far in advance of the potential problem as possible. Lenders are frequently willing to waive covenants if they can be shown how the condition will be improved or corrected.

Never put the account or loan officer of the lending institution in a situation where bad news from your company will come as a surprise. Ongoing communication with the lending institution is vital, including both good news and bad news.

By the same token, you don't have to disclose everything. The bank could misunderstand some information or become alarmed unnecessarily. An account officer may react too hastily because his or her own career is always in jeopardy for failing to spot a client company's fortunes slipping until it's too late for the bank to protect itself. Always assume that lenders will act—and react—in their own self-interest. So should you.

Two Is Better Than One

Having a meaningful relationship with at least two banks is better than one. Banks do compete for business, and that competition can result in a larger credit line for you, lower interest rates, and more favorable terms. Sometimes, the aggregate amount of credit line you can obtain from two banks is greater than the amount you could have gotten from either one alone. Collateral seems to go further too. For example, Bank X might ask for all assets as collateral for a given size loan, but if Bank Y already had the equipment as collateral for an existing loan, then Bank X might accept the remaining assets as collateral without reducing the amount of the loan it intended to give. Thus, the same total collateral supported a larger aggregate loan amount.

Even limited banking activities can be used to develop a relationship with more than one bank. You could have your general disbursement account with Bank X and your payroll and tax depository accounts with Bank Y. Using two banks may cost you a little in deposit and disbursement "float" time, but the value of the developing relationships may prove to be more significant in the long run.

Whether or not your company is a borrower, you should always monitor the status of your relationship with the banks. Are channels of communication open to the highest levels in the bank's hierarchy? Do the bank's officers respect your business? Are you comfortable with your relationship with them and with the personnel involved? If your instincts tell you that the relationship is not what you want it to be, then find a way to change it or change banks. Do so while your company continues to be a potentially attractive banking client. From the company's standpoint, a good banking relationship is a valuable asset that must be nurtured and cultivated in order to be properly harvested when the time is ripe.

The Commitment Fee Game

A bank will often charge you a fee for providing a commitment letter stating your approved line of credit and the general terms regarding that line. The fee is usually calculated as a small percentage of the proposed credit line. Frankly, it doesn't seem to make much sense to pay this fee in advance for the dubious comfort of a commitment letter. If your company is creditworthy at the time you try to borrow, you will get the loan on the best terms you can negotiate, regardless of whether or not you had earlier obtained a commitment letter. If you are not creditworthy, the commitment letter is just a worthless piece of paper.

Theoretically, one of the purposes of the commitment letter is to ensure availability of your portion of the bank's total lending capacity. While there have been rare times when banks had limited funds available to lend, if you are a good account and credit risk, you almost certainly will get your loans, even without a commitment letter.

Your Friendly Bank in Action

The following true story demonstrates that banks, with the fate of a business and the careers of many hundreds of people in its grasp, may not always be a dependable shoulder to lean on.

*

A profitable, publicly owned technology company borrowed a total of $5.2 million in demand debt from two local banks (Bank P and Bank G each provided $2.6 million) with whom it had maintained good relations for twenty years. The company accumulated the debt to finance extremely rapid growth, planning to obtain more capital through another public sale of common stock. An unexpected and severe recession hit, with the double-barreled effect of closing off the market for equities on Wall Street and sending many industries into a tailspin. The company indefinitely postponed its plans for a stock offering.

Company management anticipated a significant decline in sales (as high as 50 percent) over the next twelve months and major, unavoidable losses. The company expected a full recovery in its market to start in about eighteen months. By cutting expenses, reducing production and inventories, liquidating receivables, layoffs and salary reductions, the company expected sufficient cash flow to pay its debt interest and ride out the storm while still maintaining vital product-development programs. The company presented its forecast and plans to Bank P and Bank G, requesting they remain patient with their present demand debt position, or, alternatively, convert it to a four-year-term loan with monthly payments of $55,000 to each bank.

Bank P, without warning to the company or the other bank, immediately called its $2.6 million loan. It further demanded the company pledge its $15 million in assets as security and agree to pay $145,000 per month to Bank P over the next eighteen months or face immediate liquidation. Upon learning of Bank P's actions, Bank G made the same demands.

Rejecting the dubious alternative of voluntary bankruptcy, the company offered to pledge its assets and agreed to payments of $72,500 per month to each bank over thirty-six months. To accomplish this plan, the company would permanently abandon one-half of its product lines and cease most new product development. Both banks accepted the plan.

When the company president made the last payment to the banks some seven months ahead of schedule, the senior loan officer of Bank P offhandedly recalled the events of twenty-nine months ago.

"You know," he said, "when the loan committee met to decide on your repayment plan, half wanted to accept it and the other half wanted to force liquidation. It was a close call."

Under new leadership and panicked by the recession, Bank P had clamped down on many of its accounts. The trust and loyalty on which the borrower had depended was destroyed. Not only were many companies unnecessarily forced into ruin, but the bank itself spent years attempting to restore its relationship with the local business community.

*

Borrow if you must, but do so wisely, and be forewarned that you can never take a bank for granted. No matter how long and friendly the relationship has been, people and situations change and you may be unpleasantly surprised. The survival of your company will depend upon how well you can insulate it from the capriciousness of institutions that hold your fate in their hands.

Chapter 15

Inventory

ALMOST every company, regardless of size, has more working capital tied up in inventory than in any other current asset. In fact, the total value of raw materials, work-in-progress, and finished goods is probably greater than any other company asset. With so much capital tied up in inventory, a company cannot be cavalier about exercising tight control over the creation, movement, storage, control, and disposition of its inventory. There can be little disagreement that management's ability to select, schedule, purchase, manufacture, store, and ultimately sell its inventory according to some logical plan is vital to the survival of the company.

Good inventory management is one of the cornerstones of business survival and success. Expensive software programs exist to assist management in material requirements planning (MRP), perpetual inventory record-keeping, shop-floor loading, work-order scheduling, and myriad other administrative and manufacturing phases related to inventory management. Large mainframe computers process the inventory data and spit out reams of data and analyses. Yet, given the big investment in front-office manpower and equipment to manage the inventory, many companies usually have their lowest-paid management and support personnel in their stockroom. It's like building an Indy 500 racing car and having it serviced at the corner super-speedy lubrication center.

Who Manages the Stockroom: Penny Wise or Pound Foolish?

Check your payroll records to see how much you're paying your personnel, including supervisors and managers, assigned to the various aspects of inventory record-keeping, movement, storage, and handling. Also ask yourself if these employees are among your best and brightest. To put it another way, would you want your stockroom manager to be responsible for handling your company's cash? But there you are with the major company asset under the stockroom's control.

It may be true that your inventory records are being processed by the best computer system in the world, and you may have issued procedures and how-to manuals to cover every conceivable eventuality. But you might be surprised to find out the differences between what actually goes on in the stockroom and what data are put into the computer. There is no procedures manual that covers all the possibilities encountered in a stockroom. Putting your faith in the problem-solving abilities of a procedures manual is an invitation to chaos.

*

> Donorik Industries manufactures a system that provides automatic lubrication to critical wear points on expensive machine tools. Because the system is sold as an add-on feature to the machine tool after-market, a variety of system configurations are manufactured to retrofit a large number of different machine tool brands and types (lathes, milling machines, grinders). Business has been brisk, and Donorik is experiencing rapid growth, but the company suffers from a lack of manufacturing floor space, especially in the crowded stockroom area.
>
> Donorik maintained a computerized perpetual-inventory record-keeping system that included a "stock locator code." The code identified the aisle, rack, and bin where each part or component was stored. When a work order was released, the inventory personnel would get a print-out (pick-list) specifying the quantity and location of each part number to be pulled and delivered to the assembly floor. The system worked well for a number of years, until the stockroom became too crowded for the personnel to follow the standard operating procedures.
>
> Faced with insufficient storage space for all the additional parts, the stockroom foreman instructed his personnel to double-up on existing space. Doubling up meant that if there was no empty bin for Part #123, they could store it in any other

bin where there was room. The foreman made sure that the new bin location code for Part #123 was entered into the computer. To the hard-pressed foreman, this seemed like a reasonable and practical solution under the circumstances.

In just a few months, utter chaos reigned in the stockroom. Stock records and the procurement department indicated that certain parts were on hand in ample quantities when, in reality, supplies were short. In addition, work orders were sometimes issued for the wrong parts, or the part removed from inventory was not the part called for in the pick-list, even though it was in the right bin.

The procedure manual required that the foreman report all new location codes. What he had never been told was that the computer system was set up to handle only one location per stock item. Thus, when Part #123 came in the next time and there was no room left in the temporary bin, say #A3W," the stockroom personnel might find space in "bin #C7R," where Part #456 is located. When that transaction was reported to the computer, it would change the location code for *all* of Part #123 in stock to "bin #C7R," regardless of the multiple-storage locations of Part #123. When a pick-list asked for a quantity of Part #123, it would specify location "bin #C7R." If the pick quantity was greater than the quantity in "bin #C7R," a "shortage report" would be recorded, even though there may be hundreds of Part #123 still remaining in "bin #A3W."

The stockroom foreman had never been allowed to participate in discussions relating to the systems that interfaced with his operational area. He was expected to be just a willing workhorse who would keep those lazy bums in the stockroom moving. It was a difficult six weeks before the company's 15,000-item, $3.5 million inventory was brought back into control. Tens of thousands of dollars in production time, late deliveries, and overtime were lost. Perhaps most important, considerable customer goodwill was also lost. The moral of the story is that, in the end, Donorik Industries got just what it paid for.

*

Even if you have a clear, well-written procedures manual, do not underestimate the need for quality leadership in the stockroom and related areas (purchasing, expediting, shipping, receiving, packing, etc.). Inventory management personnel is not the place to try to do things the cheap way. If you aren't careful, you may actually get what you pay for. An alert management group recognizes that the cost of having top-grade people in inventory management may be a small price to pay for the benefits received from prompt, accurate processing of the company's largest asset.

Inventory Valuation: Management Science or Black Art?

Many privately owned firms (and probably some public firms) play games with their year-end inventory value for financial reporting purposes. Why? There are two basic reasons:

1. Reducing the inventory value has the effect of understating profits. Lowering the profits can reduce the amount of income taxes to be paid, or it can postpone the recognition of some profits until a later, more propitious time.
2. Overstating the inventory value has the effect of inflating profits and perhaps can turn around a loss situation. It also inflates the collateral value of the inventory. Either may be a desirable result if a nervous lending bank is peering over the shoulders of the company's officers.

Some companies make a regular practice of such tactics, with and without their accountants' knowledge. The reality is, given the routine accounting and auditing tests an independent accounting firm usually employs to test inventory values (in connection with certifying the financial statements), few accounting firms will be able to detect a deliberate management effort to inflate or deflate the inventory value. While subsequent events and hindsight may disclose the fraud, management's attempt to deceive has a reasonably good chance of escaping initial detection. Even if you never employ such fraudulent tactics, it is possible that a manager of one of your subsidiaries, branches, or divisions may do so.

To Confound Is to Confuse

Some companies may have so distorted their inventory valuations that the gross profit percentage in their P&L statement is meaningless as a performance measure. For example, revenue derived in the current operating period from the sales of materials deliberately omitted from last year-end's inventory valuation will mask a gross margin deterioration in the current period.

In other situations, the true cost structure of individual products (the sum of a product's component material and labor costs) bears no relationship to the aggregate carrying values in inventory, which have been manipulated to achieve some other tax or balance-sheet objective.

Where before a difference between "book inventory value" and "actual inventory value" was a matter for management to investigate, now management itself has created chaos. If management doesn't know what the inventory values should be, it will be practically impossible to detect inventory shortages, thefts, or errors created by others.

Obviously it is dangerous, if not illegal, to play games with inventory values. The moralist may wag his finger at you, while the realist may say, "You've got to do what you've got to do if you want the company to survive." The truth is, many companies do "fiddle with the books," and most of the music is played in the stockroom with inventory values.

Write-Offs and Reserves as a Management Tool

It is the rare company that doesn't have some inventory that shortly may become obsolete, stale, out of fashion, or otherwise of depreciated value. Although inventory records, physical inspection, and other systems (or accountants) may help you identify, quantify, and value such inventory, there is a great deal of subjective management judgment in determining which inventory items fall into such categories and what their remaining value, if any, should be.

Regardless of the accounting method used for valuing inventory—LIFO (last in-first out), FIFO (first in-first out), or moving average, the basic principles of accounting require that inventory be stated at the *lower* of cost or market value. (Note that "market value" in this context is defined as the anticipated selling price less all the costs yet to be incurred in completing, selling, and getting it to the customer.) In plain English, a company must immediately recognize all possible future losses that can be expected to be incurred in the ultimate sale of products now existing in inventory as finished or in-process goods.

Many companies establish balance-sheet reserves; for example, reserves for obsolete, excess, slow-moving, or damaged inventory. These are deducted from the total inventory value reflected in the balance sheet, with the contra entry made as a cost or expense on the P&L statement. These reserves are adjusted at the end of each accounting period to reflect the then-current condition of the inventory and the required reserves. (Note that most, if not all, inventory reserves are not deductible for arriving at taxable income for tax computation purposes. Because IRS regulations permit a number of special accounting treatments for tax purposes, the income reported on an annual report may be quite different from that same year's "taxable" income as reported on the tax return.)

The criteria and tests (presumably objective, but really quite subjective) used originally to identify and value the inventory items to be reserved against (and any subsequent adjustments thereto) are established and defined by management.

It is precisely the "subjective judgment" that gives management the latitude to "decide" how large the reserve should be, and thus how great the impact on reported profits and inventory values. Obviously inventory reserves created by management must have a logical, valid basis that will pass the scrutiny of the outside accountants and others, but most accounting firms are not in a position, and rarely choose to challenge, management's definition of what inventory and products will be obsolete or out of fashion next season or next year.

A company (and its stockholders) may be well served by a management that makes careful, judicious use of inventory reserves to achieve desirable, valid company objectives by carefully playing by and within the rules.

Treat the Disease, Not the Symptoms

Inventory mismanagement is a principal trigger for a financial crisis and one of the leading causes of business failure. When a company has too much and/or the "wrong stuff" in inventory, a serious domino effect begins. Almost immediately the company starts experiencing the symptoms of cash-flow pressures—stretching out suppliers, foregoing discounts for early payment, paying other, noninventory bills later and later. Even if the company has untapped sources of credit to draw upon to ease the pressure, it is merely using its rapidly dwindling supply of quick fixes instead of curing the main sickness. This disease is not the exclusive curse of unprofitable companies either. Many profitable companies mismanage their inventory too.

Tools for Self-Diagnosis

There are tools you can use to measure and monitor both the wisdom and status of your inventory investment. Each tool has a place and function in the manager's toolbox, to be used on a regular and consistent basis.

The Sales Forecast

The first tool is the sales forecast. Obviously you accumulate inventory in anticipation of the later sale of those items. Even though no sales forecast is perfect, it is still the foundation of any intelligent inventory plan. However, no matter how accurate the sales forecast, it may still entail financial commitments and requirements that are beyond the company's ability to fund with a reasonable measure of financial safety.

Average Days' Sales

Another tool is a measurement of the average number of days' sales you have in inventory. This is calculated by dividing the cost of goods sold reported in the operating statement for any given accounting period (month, quarter, or year) by the number of days in that accounting period. For example, if your cost of goods sold for last year totaled $720,000, divide that number by 360 days (most business calculations of this sort use 360 days and not 365 days) to arrive at the average cost of goods sold for a day, in this case, $2,000:

$720,000 cost of goods sold ÷ 360 days = $2,000 per day

Then divide the year-end inventory balance, say $300,000, by the $2,000 average daily cost of goods sold:

$300,000 inventory balance ÷ $2,000 per day = 150 days

The result of this calculation of the average number of days of sales carried in inventory (in this example, 150 days) indicates that you were carrying approximately 150 days worth of sales in your inventory at year-end. That number should then be compared to the length of time it takes you to procure or produce the inventory you sell. If you can usually obtain (buy or build) the inventory you need in, say, 45 days, then you have about 105 days more supply of inventory on hand than you probably need.

Inventory Turnover Rate

Another business measurement tool you should use is the calculation of your inventory turnover rate. While this computation can be made using the year-end inventory balance only, it is considerably more meaningful if you are able to use the value of the inventory at several dates during the year, especially if there are significant seasonal variations in sales and/or inventory, or there is a big difference between beginning and ending inventories in the year. If, for example, the inventory investment measured at the end of each quarter averaged $240,000, then by dividing that number into the cost of goods sold for the year, say, $720,000, you will see that the inventory turnover rate was three times a year.

While dollars are used in the calculation, the practical implication is that each inventory item was put into, then sold out of, inventory three times during the year. Obviously this is only a general overall measurement. Some inventory items may have turned over only once, if at all, while others may have turned over six or seven times. However, the average turnover-rate calculation is a useful measurement and indicator of the effectiveness of inventory planning and scheduling.

Perpetual Inventory Records

Perpetual inventory records are not the easiest or cheapest records to maintain, but they can provide valuable and useful inventory information. Properly administered perpetual records tell you what and how much of each item is supposed to be in stock at any given point. These records are an excellent basis for doing test counts and obsolescence reviews, as well as for calculating total inventory investment and detecting shortages and theft. In addition, they can provide usage, turnover, and consumption data on a per-item basis. Computerization of the perpetual records can improve the processing and accuracy of stockroom transactions, but the system will still depend on how well the stockroom personnel do their job in preparing the raw input data.

Before you use these various management tools, you must acknowledge certain business realities that will impinge upon your ability to manage your inventory. Among these realities are:

1. The purchase or manufacture of inventory for sale by the company requires a period of lead time before that inventory is available to you. This means your company must make financial commitments significantly in advance of knowing what your incoming orders will be.

2. How much you order or build of a given item will have a significant effect upon your unit cost of that item. Since the lower the unit cost, the greater the gross margin, there is always pressure from certain segments of the company to seek the lowest cost.

Cost is only one of the factors you must consider in making inventory decisions. The interaction of lead times, economic order quantities, safety stock, reorder points, manufacturing yields, waste, and other considerations must be factored into the inventory decision process. Haphazard ordering practices, such as ordering inappropriate quantities, will create havoc with your total inventory investment and send shock waves throughout the company.

3. A business experiencing sales growth usually requires an increasing inventory investment and additional working capital. While improving the inventory turnover rate of a given inventory investment can support a higher sales volume at the same working capital level, you must ultimately expect to have more funds tied up in inventory as you grow.

4. A time delay between the date you ship the product and the date you receive payment from the customer is inescapable. Each industry or market has its own more or less standard terms that you must abide by. Regardless of the payment terms you specify on your invoice, say net 30 days, if the industrywide average collection period is 45 days, then that, and perhaps an additional small cushion, is what you should include in your planning. All other things being equal, the longer the collection period, the less funds you will have available to invest in inventory if you hope to maintain fiscal stability.

5. Practically every measurement tool used by management deals in averages or takes a broad, overall look. As valuable and useful as these tools are, they are no substitute for reviewing the individual items that comprise the aggregate inventory. Even though one or more measurements of the "average" may indicate satisfactory performance, unquestionably some portions of your inventory are not being well managed. To this end, the perpetual inventory records can be invaluable in helping you improve your profitability, cash flow, and rate of return.

Chapter 16

P&L Analysis: A Management Necessity

SUPPOSE your company had just completed its fiscal year and you were reviewing the results: sales up 13 percent and net after-tax profits up 12 percent over the prior year's results. The company is now earning 9 percent net profit on every sales dollar, slightly lower than the 10 percent rate of profit in the prior year. What would your first thought be about how to increase profits in the next year?

To begin with, a surprisingly large number of capable executives would be quite satisfied with the recent 9 percent return. More than likely, those same executives would see another reduction in the rate of profit the following year as a direct result of their complacent management response.

MORE, MORE, MORE!

When the pressure to earn greater profits is removed, the existing rate of profits usually erodes. This doesn't mean you have to turn into a greedy, tight-fisted Simon Legree who continually pounds on the desk screaming "More, more, more!" It does mean you must keep everyone aware that profit improvement is an ongoing objective of your management team; that being content is the first sign of going backwards. However, unless you match the profit improvement goal with a rewards distribution system that will have a positive impact on everyone's compensation or benefit package as the objectives are being accomplished, the constant pressure will have the reverse effect and destroy morale and performance.

Often a deteriorating *rate of profitability* is obscured or overlooked in the euphoria of earning greater aggregate profit dollars. The decline in the rate of profit earned on sales from 10 percent to 9 percent requires a serious investigation and detailed explanation. The possible causes of such a performance may have unrealized importance. For example, suppose the handful of products that generated the 13 percent increase in sales was enormously profitable, while the rest of the sales—the major portion of your products—suffered significant erosion in profitability through lower sales prices or higher costs. Perhaps selling costs got out of control because of expensive programs to boost sales of the least profitable products. The point is, a decreasing rate of profitability is an important symptom under any conditions.

Almost invariably, the first, and unfortunately the only, place on which management concentrates in an effort to increase profits is the sales revenue area, almost totally ignoring the other part of the equation—costs and expenses. Perhaps when business slows down and things get tougher, management will turn to cutting expenses in a belated effort to regain or revitalize profitability.

Obviously, increasing sales revenue is an important objective for many reasons, but it is not the only way to maintain and enhance profitability in good times, bad times, or average times. Whatever your rate of profits or total earnings, you must not allow yourself or any of your executives to back off from a stable program of expense containment and control that provides a complete justification for all costs.

THE OPEN BARN DOOR

The profit-and-loss statement is the second place to look when doing profit analysis. The first is the budget you prepared before the start of the period being analyzed. Obviously no budget is a perfect forecast of future events and results, but if you forged the budget based on sound fundamentals and procedures (see Chapter 9), it should closely approximate what ultimately will be reported on the P&L statement. Waiting until the period is over before you approve the level and composition of costs and expenses to be incurred is the same thing as locking the barn door too late.

One of the first mistakes top management makes is to look only at the summary or top schedule of the P&L statement or budget. Unless you take the time to delve into the nitty-gritty of costs, expenses, revenues, and margins, you will consistently remain in the dark and miss the mark in your search for profit improvement.

The process of preparing the P&L statement is actually a series of categorizations and accumulations of detailed expenses and costs that start at the individual account level of the chart of accounts system, with subtotals moving forward to represent increasingly larger expense categories and/or company functions. By the time the P&L statement is prepared, practically every cost and expense component has lost its singular identity and is now grouped into a small handful of overall categories. Few top managers and even fewer members of the board of directors take the time to review and understand the detailed composition of the operating statement.

Exhibit 16.1 is a typical P&L statement that might be submitted to top management. While this is an accurate reflection of the company's performance, it provides only a minimum of data for doing a profit analysis.

The Accounting System

Unless a company has taken the trouble to install, debug, and implement a flexible, detailed accounting system, analysis will be difficult and time-consuming, perhaps almost impossible. Many excellent computer software programs are available that provide the framework for the accounting system (chart of accounts, general and subsidiary ledgers, trial balances, reports, statements, analyses), but you still cannot escape the need for trained personnel to do the timely, accurate coding and processing of the raw input data (invoices, vouchers, checks, payroll data, bills) according to some rigid and consistent rules. The sophistication of your general accounting system, cost-accounting system, inventory records, and other subsystems, plus the structure of your organization, will determine the degree of meaningful financial analysis and information you can obtain.

Another factor that management frequently underestimates is the difficulty for most accounting systems to adapt to frequent changes in the company's organizational structure. Every time a department is shifted or created (for example, an independent marketing department is carved out of the existing sales department), the accounting system has to be able to include the new department without invalidating the existing chart of accounts. Also, for accurate comparison and analysis purposes in the future, certain historical data from prior periods will

Exhibit 16.1
A Typical P&L Statement

ANYCOMPANY, INC.
Summary of Operations

	For the Year Ended December 31	
	1988	*1987*
Net sales	$2,100,000	$1,900,000
Costs and expenses:		
Cost of goods sold	975,000	850,000
Depreciation & amortization	120,000	105,000
Research expenses	175,000	145,000
Selling expenses	385,000	305,000
General and administrative expenses	215,000	195,000
Total costs and expenses	1,870,000	1,600,000
Income from operations	230,000	300,000
Net interest (expense)	(110,000)	(90,000)
Income before income taxes	120,000	210,000
Provision for income taxes	50,000	96,000
Net income	70,000	114,000

have to be deleted from the sales department's expense statements and reflected in those of the new marketing department.

A new accounting system is expensive to install and often requires six months to a year before it is completed. Because the accounting system used is vital if you want prompt, accurate financial statements, budgets, and related analysis, you must take a long-range view when considering a new or revised system for your company. To select a system that cannot accommodate your company as it grows in size and complexity can be an unfortunate mistake.

WHO DOES THE ANALYSIS?

Since, at last look, most executives are human beings, with all the usual human foibles and idiosyncracies, no one likes to put oneself on the carpet by voluntarily pointing out where he or she "blew the budget." Because the senior officer of the company probably doesn't have the time to do a detailed, in-depth profit analysis, he must establish a system of procedures and methods so that it is performed in a timely and standard manner. Accordingly, the chief financial officer (CFO) of the company, whatever his or her title may be, is usually delegated as coordinator of the process, and may provide the other officers and executives with much of the raw data needed to perform the analysis.

At the least, the senior manager should require an explanation of any revenue or expense category that deviates from the budget plan by some fixed percentage, as specified by the senior manager. How large or small that percentage should be will vary depending on the size and financial performance of the company, the detail available in the chart of accounts, how many and which accounts are involved, and other factors, not the least of which is the willingness of the senior officer to spend the time required to do an effective review. Certainly, any account should be reviewed that deviates from the budget by plus or minus five percent or more. In other accounts, a deviation of as small as one percent could involve a significant amount of money.

A good way to approach the problem of what to review is to use a combined approach, requiring an analysis and explanation of:

1. Certain designated accounts regardless of their deviation from budget.
2. Any account that has a deviation of plus or minus a certain percentage.
3. Any account where the dollar difference, plus or minus, exceeds a certain dollar amount.

Frequently, the CFO is responsible for explaining the variations between budgeted and actual results for all departments and activities. While the CFO may have the numbers at his fingertips and can highlight the various accounts meeting the "must be analyzed criteria," it is a mistake to make the CFO responsible for justifying departmental performance not under his or her direct control. Each executive must be held responsible for the performance and expenses of the areas they control and all deviations from the plan.

Certainly some deviations will involve multidepartmental interactions, and thus there may be some finger-pointing among the executives. Sales may argue that it exceeded its budget for field-service travel expenses because the manufacturing department was shipping products requiring greater-than-anticipated warranty claims and repairs. Or manufacturing may claim that it incurred extra overtime expense because the blueprints and specifications received from engineering were faulty, and so forth. At the least, executives will recognize their interdependence and mutual need for constant communication.

The process of comparing actual performance to budget or forecast can be a time of constructive tension among the executive group, if the senior officer handles it correctly. It can also result in bitter encounters, leading to permanent animosities and conflicts among members of the executive group. You will want to have both individual and group review sessions with your executives. When you meet, *you* must set and maintain the tone for the process, being diplomatic in your criticisms, questions, and comments. Under no circumstances should you censure an executive in a group session.

Where Did We Go Wrong?

In most cases, budgets are missed as a result of four basic situations, not because of executive carelessness or spendthrift behavior:

1. The failure of the forecast/budget to have anticipated or allowed for the general business conditions or environment of the company.
2. The failure to have recognized a problem in the company's products, processes, or personnel that existed at the time the forecast/budget was prepared.
3. The failure, during the period, to modify and adjust the forecast/budget in light of any sudden problems or changing conditions.
4. The failure to have created a unity of purpose, teamwork, and an attitude of caring among the human resources of the company.

Reviewing and comparing budget and actual results is an educational process, not a punishment exercise. Its purposes are to learn what went wrong and why, what was right and why, and how the company's performance can be improved in the future. It can be one of the most practical and effective functions you perform.

Chapter 17

An Approach to P&L Analysis

ONE of the first steps in P&L budgeting and the subsequent analysis of results is to recognize certain profit-and-loss fundamentals:

1. All costs do not change in direct proportion to changes in revenue.
2. All costs do not change at the same rate or as a result of the same stimuli.
3. Profits do not change in direct proportion to either costs or revenue.

The proof of those fundamentals is simple: If your sales increased 10 percent, would your profits also increase 10 percent? Obviously not. Some costs will be affected by the increase in revenue (such as sales commissions and shipping costs), while others will not (depreciation, rent). Only by analyzing and understanding the causative factors and relationships that can affect individual costs and revenues will you and management be able to anticipate, plan, and exercise some control of profit.

Fixed, Variable, Semivariable, and Discretionary Costs

Although the concept of fixed, variable, and semivariable costs has traditionally been considered in connection with cost accounting and the manufacturing department, almost every cost or expense in a company, regardless of the department involved, fits into one of four categories. Understanding the internal and external forces that cause a specific cost to increase or decrease is the first step to being able to exercise control over that cost.

Fixed Costs

Fixed costs (sometimes called "period costs") usually cannot be changed in the short term. This does not mean that fixed costs are beyond management's control, but rather that *within the time period being considered*, management's ability to reduce or eliminate them is limited. Depreciation and rent are typical examples, but others, such as utility costs (light, heat, and electricity), may be considered fixed because only a small portion of the total expense would be affected by changes in revenue or production during the current period.

Variable Costs

Variable costs are those in which a significant portion of the costs to be incurred are directly proportional to revenue generated or the production rate during the period. In fact, such costs may not be incurred in the absence of production or revenue. Sometimes called "direct costs" because of the relationship with production or revenue generation, production labor and materials are the usual examples, but others may include such things as freight out and sales commissions.

Semivariable Costs

Semivariable costs have no direct relationship to revenue or production volume and are essentially fixed, but some additional portion of the costs may be affected by changes in revenue, production, or management action. By far, most costs and expenses in the typical company can be classified as semivariable. For example, if you operate a retail store, the cost for the sales clerks is essentially fixed, although if business exceeds expectations, you might have to add a sales clerk or two to handle the increased volume, or let one or two go if business is slow. Or, some payroll fringe costs have a fixed element to them, such as monthly health insurance premiums based on predetermined per-person rates, but the cost will vary according to the *number* of employees.

Discretionary Costs

Discretionary costs do not relate to revenue or production at all, and they are totally within management's power to influence directly.

Charitable contributions is the obvious example. Bonuses sometimes fit in this category, as do some advertising and public relations expenses.

Accurate budgeting, controlling expenditures, and analyzing actual performance correctly depend upon understanding these four types of costs. Merely analyzing and comparing numbers without at the same time considering internal and external forces, management decisions, and interaccount relationships that affect revenue and expenses won't tell you what you need to know. You don't have to be a CPA to interpret financial statements; you just need to exercise some logic and use common business sense.

Take It from the Top

Although the preparation of P&L statements is a "from the bottom-up" accounting process, the analysis and review process is "from the top down." The type of information reported in Exhibit 16.1 is shown in a more useful and informative format in Exhibit 17.1. Although Exhibits 17.1 through 17.3 relating to the Hypothetical Technology Company are reflected on an annual basis, you should have similar comparative statements prepared at least quarterly: first quarter; first and second quarter presented individually and year to date; first, second, and third quarter presented individually and year to date; and first, second, third, and fourth quarter presented individually and year to date. You will also want to refer to the prior year's financial data for the same period.

Exhibit 17.1, a two-year comparative statement, reflects each line item as a percentage of net sales (provision for taxes is shown as a percentage of pretax income) and creates four new lines: gross sales, returns and allowances, gross profit, and total operating expenses.

Almost immediately, important questions jump off the page. Why did returns and allowances almost double? What caused the gross profit margin to deteriorate? What is behind the increase in selling expenses? Using percentages in the financial reports, although just a simple change, is the first step to gaining greater insight into what happened. Often looking at the dollars alone won't help. Percentage analysis may provide a clearer, more useful look at relationships and ratios.

As part of the "from the top down" analysis process, the top P&L schedule must be supported by certain other schedules that present supplementary information to help you interpret the results.

Exhibit 17.2 provides a quarterly look at the recent annual results

Exhibit 17.1
HYPOTHETICAL TECHNOLOGY COMPANY
Comparative Summary of Operations

	For the Year Ended December 31			
	1988		*1987*	
	$	%	*$*	%
Gross sales	8,290,000	108.3	7,550,000	106.3
Returns and allowances	690,000	8.3	450,000	6.3
Net sales	7,600,000	100.0	7,100,000	100.0
Cost of goods sold	3,610,000	47.5	3,230,000	45.5
Gross profit	3,990,000	52.5	3,970,000	54.5
Operating expenses:				
Depreciation and amortization	433,000	5.7	390,000	5.5
Research expense	633,000	8.3	540,000	7.6
Selling expense	1,391,000	18.3	1,143,000	16.1
General and administrative expense	775,000	10.2	731,000	10.3
Total operating expenses	3,232,000	42.5	2,804,000	39.5
Income from operations	758,000	10.0	1,066,000	15.0
Net interest expense	255,000	3.4	110,000	1.5
Income before income taxes	503,000	3.6	956,000	13.5
Provision for taxes	200,000	40.0	478,000	50.0
Net income	303,000	3.9	478,000	6.7

and includes a comparison with the budgets for each of the four quarters.

Note that there is no column in Exhibit 17.2 that gives a total of the four quarterly budgets to compare with the actual annual results. Unless you prepared a budget for the entire year at the beginning of the year, you shouldn't try to use the total of the individual quarterly budgets made during the year as a substitute. Here's the reason:

Suppose you included $50,000 in the first-quarter budget for a special engineering project, but, one month into the first quarter, you

Exhibit 17.2

Anycompany, Inc.
Comparison Of Actual And Budgeted Results By Quarters
For The Year 1988
,000 Omitted

	First Quarter Ending March 31						Second Quarter Ending June 30					
	Actual		Budget		Over (Under)		Actual		Budget		Over (Under)	
	$	%	$	%	$	%	$	%	$	%	$	%
Gross Sales	1,900	108.6	1,850	102.7	50	2.7	1,960	105.9	1,950	102.6	10	0.5
Returns And Allowances	150	8.6	50	2.7	100	300.0	110	5.9	50	2.6	60	120.0
Net Sales	1,750	100.0	1,800	100.0	(50)	(2.8)	1,850	100.0	1,900	100.0	(50)	(2.6)
Cost Of Goods Sold:												
Beginning Inventory	3,900		3,900				4,120		4,120			
Quarter's Activity:												
Material Purchases	183		100		83	83.0	130		100		30	30.0
Direct Labor	238		210		28	13.3	240		220		20	9.1
Factory Overhead	600		550		50	9.1	610		575		35	6.1
Freight In/Out	55		50		5	10.0	60		50		10	20.0
Quarter's Total Input	1076		910		166	18.2	1040		945		95	10.1
Inventory Adjustments	(25)		-		(25)	100.0	(350)		-		(350)	100.0
Total Goods Available	4,951		4,810		141	2.9	4,810		5,065		(255)	(5.0)
Ending Inventory	4,120		4,000		120	3.0	3,913		4,210		(297)	(7.1)
Cost Of Goods Sold	831	47.5	810	45.0	21	2.6	897	48.5	855	45.0	42	4.9
Gross Profit	919	52.5	990	55.0	(71)	(7.2)	953	51.5	1,045	55.0	(92)	(8.8)
Operating Expenses:												
Depreciation And Amort'n	95	5.4	90	5.0	5	5.6	105	5.7	95	5.0	10	10.5
Research Expense	140	8.0	160	8.9	(20)	(12.5)	158	8.5	160	8.4	(2)	1.3
Selling Expense	280	16.0	250	13.9	30	12.0	310	16.8	275	14.5	35	10.9
Gen'l and Admin. Expense	163	9.3	155	8.6	8	4.9	174	9.4	160	8.4	14	8.8
Total Operating Expenses	678	38.7	655	36.4	23	3.5	747	40.4	690	36.3	57	8.3
Income From Operations	241	13.8	335	18.6	(94)	(28.0)	206	11.1	355	18.7	(149)	(42.0)
Net Interest Expense	40	2.3	35	1.9	5	14.3	65	3.5	40	2.1	25	62.5
Income Before Taxes	201	11.5	300	16.7	99	33.3	141	7.6	315	16.6	(124)	(39.4)

	Third Quarter Ending September 30						Fourth Quarter Ending December 31					
	Actual		Budget		Over (Under)		Actual		Budget		Over (Under)	
	$	%	$	%	$	%	$	%	$	%	$	%
Gross Sales	2,110	111.1	2,075	103.8	35	1.7	2,320	110.5	2,075	103.8	245	11.8
Returns And Allowances	210	11.1	75	3.8	135	180.0	220	10.5	75	3.8	145	193.3
Net Sales	1,900	100.0	2,000	100.0	(100)	(5.0)	2,100	100.0	2,000	100.0	100	5.0
Cost Of Goods Sold:												
Beginning Inventory	3,913		3,913				4,117		4,117			
Quarter's Activity:												
Material Purchases	150		125		25	20.0	135		150		(15)	(10.0)
Direct Labor	250		255		(5)	(2.0)	230		225		5	2.2
Factory Overhead	650		675		(25)	(3.7)	630		650		(20)	(3.1)
Freight In/Out	100		55		45	81.8	100		55		45	81.8
Quarter's Total Input	1150		1110		40	3.6	1095		1080		15	1.4
Inventory Adjustments	-		-		-	-	-		-		-	-
Total Goods Available	5,063		5,023		40	0.8	5,212		5,197		15	0.3
Ending Inventory	4,117		4,083		34	0.8	4,276		4,297		(21)	(0.5)
Cost Of Goods Sold	946	49.8	940	47.0	6	0.6	936	44.6	900	45.0	36	4.0
Gross Profit	954	50.2	1,160	53.0	(206)	(12.9)	1,164	55.4	1,100	55.0	64	5.8
Operating Expenses:												
Depreciation And Amort'n	113	5.9	110	5.5	3	2.7	120	5.7	110	5.5	10	9.1
Research Expense	165	8.7	160	8.0	5	3.1	170	8.1	175	8.8	(5)	(2.9)
Selling Expense	390	20.5	350	17.5	40	11.4	411	19.6	350	17.5	61	17.4
Gen'l and Admin. Expense	218	11.5	200	10.0	18	9.0	220	10.5	200	10.0	20	10.0
Total Operating Expenses	886	46.6	820	41.0	66	8.0	921	43.9	835	41.8	86	10.3
Income From Operations	68	3.6	340	17.0	(272)	(80.0)	243	11.5	265	13.2	(22)	(8.3)
Net Interest Expense	66	3.5	60	3.0	6	10.0	84	4.0	65	3.2	19	29.2
Income Before Taxes	2	0.1	280	14.0	(278)	99.3	159	7.5	200	10.0	(41)	(20.5)

realize the project will have to be delayed until sometime in the third quarter. When it's time to budget the third quarter, you include the $50,000 in the third quarter's budget. If, at the end of the year, you use the total of the four quarters' budgets to arrive at an annual budget, you will have included the $50,000 project budget twice, unless you remembered to go back and restate the first quarter's budget.

The same situation could occur with an advertising campaign or a major repair and maintenance program, where a delay requires that the expenditure be rebudgeted in a later quarter. Because many of these items, big and small, happen every quarter, it becomes almost impossible to track them in order to restate a prior quarter's budget. Thus, the total of the four individual quarter's budgets is *not* the same as an annual budget.

A Sample Analysis

You are the new COO of Hypothetical Technology Company, a six-year-old manufacturer of electronically controlled home and office humidifiers and dehumidifiers. You have asked the accounting department to prepare a series of financial statements, summaries, and comparisons for your review. You have already reviewed the summary information in Exhibit 17.1 and are now reviewing Exhibit 17.2. What operating, budgeting, and financial questions can you develop as a result of reviewing the information in Exhibit 17.2?

At First Glance

A partial list of questions raised by the information presented in Exhibit 17.2 would include:

Gross Sales

You have been able to forecast your gross sales with reasonable accuracy, at least in aggregate dollars, although the fourth-quarter forecast was off by 11.8 percent. If the detailed composition of the sales forecast was as accurate as the total dollars forecasted have been, the manufacturing department's job of scheduling and achieving on-budget production should have been relatively easy. Review the details of the product mix, as well as the pricing and discount policy.

Returns and Allowances

Your company has consistently underestimated sales returns and allowances. This raises several important questions: Why has the forecast been so difficult to predict, and why was such a large amount estimated in the first place? Is there a product quality or pricing problem? This important symptom requires further investigation.

Net Sales

Cost of Goods Sold

The details of the composition of the cost of goods sold indicate a number of potentially serious problems:

1. If the sales forecast has been accurate, why have the material purchases been so misbudgeted? Are the company's purchasing practices appropriate? Are the pricing methods reliable? Are the bills of material for the products correct? What cost-accounting system is being used? Is inventory being wasted or stolen?
2. The direct labor budget has also been consistently wrong, although it has been more accurate in recent quarters. Why was it so difficult to budget labor cost accurately early in the year? Are methods, training, and equipment adequate?
3. Factory overhead was underestimated earlier in the year, but like direct labor cost, it seems to be more accurately budgeted in the second half of the year. Is there an appropriate relationship between direct labor and materials purchases? Between direct labor and factory overhead? How is factory overhead allocated to or absorbed by production in the cost-accounting system?
4. What factors influence the amount of freight in/out? Why has that cost increased so dramatically in the third and fourth quarter, and why has it been so inaccurately budgeted?
5. The inventory adjustments in the first and especially the second quarter raise a number of questions. What were the adjustments for? Was inventory missing, scrapped, or declared obsolete? Had prior inventories been miscounted or improperly valued? How frequently is a physical inventory count done? How is the inventory valued?

If you cannot answer these questions easily, you will begin to see why the company has had difficulty achieving its targeted cost of goods sold. Then perhaps you can indicate ways to reduce those costs.

Gross Profit Margin

Since the gross profit margin is derived from the difference between sales and the cost of goods sold, analyzing gross sales, returns and allowances, net sales, and cost of goods sold will help you understand how to raise that margin.

Operating Expenses

Since operating expenses are for the most part made up primarily of fixed and semivariable expenses, they should become a smaller percentage of sales as sales increase. Instead, the total of the various operating expenses is consuming an increasingly larger portion of revenues (both as a percentage and in dollars), an undesirable situation that will require careful study. Take a look at the following situations:

1. Depreciation and amortization expenses are usually easy to budget accurately; however, the company consistently seems to underbudget that expense. In all probability, it is not taking the depreciation of the most recent quarter's asset acquisitions into account when it prepares the next quarter's budget. This should raise a larger question regarding the review and approval process for asset procurement.

2. The company devotes a significant portion of its revenues to research. Given the nature of research, it is often difficult to judge in the short-term whether value is being received for the level of expenditures made. While it appears the research department has been operating close to budget in the aggregate, a more detailed investigation will need to be done. Within the research department, a complete project cost-accounting system should be maintained in order to track how much is being spent on each project and what results are being achieved.

3. What is the typical ratio of selling expenses to sales for your market(s)? Selling expenses seem to be out of control. Not only have the budgeted expenses been climbing regularly from approximately 14 percent of sales to almost 18 percent, but the company has been exceeding this already high percentage. Further analysis of the accounts comprising selling expenses must be given a high priority (see Exhibit 17.3).

4. The aggregate dollars, as well as the percentage spent for general and administrative expenses, have been increasing steadily. Usually, as a company's sales volume increases, its general and administrative expenses decline as a percentage of sales.

Income from Operations

Income from operations, the difference between gross profit and operating expenses, has not reached its budget in any quarter. Is the company trying to achieve a definite goal in operating profits? A specific profit objective is vital in order to provide all management levels with the discipline necessary to exercise control over cost and expense budgets and establish priorities.

Net Interest Expense

Net interest expense has been increasing and also has been consistently underbudgeted. Is the company accurately forecasting its borrowing needs? What is driving the need for more borrowing? Are there untapped alternatives to borrowing or possibilities for cheaper refinancing? Has the company been underestimating the interest rate it will pay, or has it been overestimating the interest it earns on its investments?

Income Before Taxes

Income before taxes were practically nonexistent in the third quarter, when the company essentially broke even. In that quarter, cost of goods sold was exceptionally high, even though there did not seem to be any inventory adjustments. Every category of operating expense and interest expense exceeded its budget. Although sales were marginally higher than budget, the company was unable to show improved results. An in-depth review of the third quarter, especially in the manufacturing department, may provide some insight into the company's basic problems.

A Deeper Look at Operating Expenses

The issues relating to gross profit, cost of goods sold, and sales revenue are discussed in greater detail in Chapter 19. The information obtained from the review of Exhibit 17.2 has raised concerns regarding the level of various budgeted and actual operating expenses. To have a better understanding of such expenses, you will have to do an in-depth review of each category as incurred on a departmental basis. The format used in Exhibit 17.3 provides a detailed analysis of the total selling expenses for the year. The same type of schedule and analysis can and should be used for the operating expense of the other depart-

Exhibit 17.3

Hypothetical Technology Company
Comparison Of Actual And Budgeted Selling Expenses By Quarters
For The Year 1988
,000 Omitted

	First Quarter Ending March 31						Second Quarter Ending June 30					
	Actual		Budget		Over (Under)		Actual		Budget		Over (Under)	
	$	%	$	%	$	%	$	%	$	%	$	%
Salaries:												
Salaries - supervision	25	8.9	25	10.0	-	-	25	6.4	25	9.6	-	-
Salaries - field sales	42	15.0	35	14.0	7	20.0	49	12.6	42	16.2	7	20.0
Salaries - service	36	12.9	30	12.0	6	20.0	42	10.8	36	13.8	6	20.0
Salaries - sales administration	9	3.2	9	3.6	-	-	9	2.3	9	3.5	-	-
Total salaries	112	40.0	99	39.6	13	13.1	125	32.1	112	43.1	13	11.6
Payroll Fringes:												
Health insurance premium	18	6.4	15	6.0	3	20.0	20	5.1	18	6.9	2	11.1
Life insurance premium	2	0.7	2	0.8	-	-	2	0.5	2	0.8	-	-
FICA taxes - employer's share	8	2.9	7	2.8	1	14.3	9	2.3	8	3.1	1	14.3
Total payroll fringes	28	10.0	24	9.6	4	16.7	31	7.9	28	10.8	3	10.7
Departmental expenses:												
Depreciation expense - autos	6	2.1	6	2.4	-	-	6	1.5	6	2.3	-	-
Depreciation expense - office equip.	4	1.4	4	1.6	-	-	4	1.0	4	1.5	-	-
Rent	3	1.1	3	1.2	-	-	3	0.8	3	1.2	-	-
Light, heat & power	2	0.7	2	0.8	-	-	2	0.5	2	0.8	-	-
Telephone	10	3.6	10	4.0	-	-	10	2.6	10	3.8	-	-
Insurance expense	5	1.8	5	2.0	-	-	5	1.3	5	1.9	-	-
Repairs and maintenance	1	0.4	9	3.6	(8)	(88.8)	12	3.1	9	3.5	3	33.3
Advertising expense	53	18.9	50	20.0	3	0.5	60	15.4	30	11.5	30	100.0
Salesmen's travel expense	26	9.3	15	6.0	11	73.3	24	6.2	20	7.7	4	20.0
Servicemen's travel expense	32	11.4	15	6.0	17	113.3	30	7.7	24	9.2	6	25.0
Office supplies expense	3	1.1	3	1.2	-	-	3	0.8	3	1.2	-	-
Miscellaneous selling expense	5	1.8	5	2.0	-	-	5	1.3	4	1.5	1	25.0
Total departmental expenses	150	53.6	127	50.8	23	18.1	164	42.1	120	46.2	44	36.7
Total selling expense	290	103.6	250	100.0	40	16.0	320	82.1	260	100.0	60	23.1

	Third Quarter Ending September 30						Fourth Quarter Ending December 31						Total Actual For The Year
	Actual		Budget		Over (Under)		Actual		Budget		Over (Under)		
	$	%	$	%	$	%	$	%	$	%	$	%	$
Salaries:													
Salaries - supervision	25	6.2	25	9.1	-	-	25	6.1	25	9.1	-	-	100
Salaries - field sales	56	13.9	49	17.8	7	14.3	56	13.6	49	17.8	7	14.3	203
Salaries - service	48	11.9	42	15.3	6	14.3	54	13.1	42	15.3	12	28.6	180
Salaries - sales administration	9	2.2	9	3.3	-	-	12	2.9	9	3.3	3	33.3	39
Total salaries	138	34.2	125	35.7	13	10.4	147	35.6	125	35.7	22	17.6	522
Payroll Fringes:													
Health insurance premium	22	5.5	20	7.3	2	10.0	24	5.8	20	7.3	4	10.0	84
Life insurance premium	3	0.7	2	0.7	1	50.0	3	0.7	2	0.7	1	50.0	10
FICA taxes - employer's share	10	2.5	9	3.3	1	11.1	10	2.4	9	3.3	1	11.1	37
Total payroll fringes	35	8.7	31	8.9	4	12.9	37	9.0	31	8.9	6	19.4	131
Departmental expenses:													
Depreciation expense - autos	8	2.0	6	2.2	2	33.3	8	1.9	6	2.2	2	33.3	28
Depreciation expense - office equip.	5	1.2	4	1.5	1	25.0	5	1.2	4	1.5	1	25.0	18
Rent	3	0.7	3	1.1	-	-	3	0.7	3	1.1	-	-	12
Light, heat & power	2	0.5	2	0.7	-	-	2	0.5	2	0.7	-	-	8
Telephone	14	3.5	14	5.1	-	-	14	3.4	14	5.1	-	-	48
Insurance expense	5	1.2	5	1.8	-	-	5	1.2	5	1.8	-	-	20
Repairs and maintenance	2	0.5	2	0.7	-	-	2	0.5	2	0.7	-	-	17
Advertising expense	80	19.9	70	25.5	10	14.3	80	19.4	70	25.5	10	14.3	273
Salesmen's travel expense	45	11.2	35	12.7	10	28.6	50	12.1	35	12.7	15	42.9	145
Servicemen's travel expense	45	11.2	40	14.5	5	12.5	58	14.0	40	14.5	18	45.0	165
Office supplies expense	8	2.0	4	1.5	4	100.0	4	1.0	4	1.5	-	-	18
Miscellaneous selling expense	13	3.2	9	3.3	4	44.4	9	2.2	9	3.3	-	-	32
Total departmental expenses	230	57.1	194	55.4	36	18.6	240	58.1	194	55.4	46	23.7	784
Total selling expense	403	100.0	350	100.0	53	15.1	424	102.7	350	100.0	74	21.1	1437

ments (such as research expenses, general and administrative). The executive responsible for each operational area should provide you with complete answers and justification for the expenses and costs incurred by his or her department.

Rarely does an executive get approval for all the resources he or she would like to have. Sometimes an executive is caught in a bind: Solving problems or accomplishing goals may require more resources than have been budgeted or authorized. Some executives disregard budgetary considerations and instead place greater priority on solving the problem or accomplishing the mission. There is much to admire in that management style, but it is dangerous to continue to do this except in the most unusual, emergency crises. Obviously, you must balance the budgeted resources assigned to a department against its mission. Equally important is to keep channels of communication open between yourself and any executive who needs greater resources to solve a problem.

When reviewing a department's detailed expenses, do it from a larger, companywide perspective. Often the underlying source of a particular department's problems—exceeding budget, failure to meet objectives, poor morale—may be found *outside* the department. This ripple effect may create unexpected repercussions that at first glance might not be easy to identify. In short, the problem may be far removed from the symptoms.

A Departmental Review

Exhibit 17.3 provides a detailed breakdown of why and where the sales department has consistently exceeded its increasing budget. As highlighted in Exhibits 17.1 and 17.2, the sales department is consuming a large and increasing percentage of revenue. Under normal circumstances, selling expenses, as a percentage of sales revenue, should decline as sales volume increases. Reviewing the sales department's expenses may provide some information, but a complete study of the company's sales, service, and distribution system may be necessary. There may be fundamental and expensive weaknesses in the way the company deals with its market, uses its sales personnel, or provides service to its customers.

Salaries

In each of the four quarters, in spite of increases in the budget, the department has gone over budget in field sales and service salaries. That increase in salary expense has not been matched by a similar increase in sales. Of special concern is the increase in service salaries. Has the demand for increased service personnel been caused by a deterioration in product quality? Is there any relationship between the high level of sales returns and allowances and the need for more service personnel? This may be one example where an apparent budgetary problem in one department, in this case the selling department, may have its roots in another department, perhaps within the manufacturing department.

Payroll Fringes

These expenses, while over budget, seem to be directly related to and caused by the higher salary expenses.

Departmental Expenses

With the exception of advertising and travel expenses, most of the departmental expenses seem to be reasonably close to or within budget.

Advertising expenses, however, are consistently over budget, and by large amounts. What is the marketing rationale behind the advertising program? How is the budget for advertising developed—quarterly and annually?

Travel expenses for both sales and service personnel are growing. While some of the increases are due to an increase in personnel, they seem high—almost equaling salary cost. Does the company have a definitive policy regarding the authorization and reimbursement of travel expenses? Are the sales and service personnel based in appropriate locations relative to the customers they are required to serve? Do frequent problems with the quality of the products shipped demand an excessive amount of after-sale service? Does or should the company charge for service?

Reviewing a department's expenses will not provide all the answers, or even all the questions, but, when done regularly and carefully, a review has great value as a method of control. Since time is a precious commodity for a business executive, it is understandable that management tends to concentrate on variances or deviations from plan. Nevertheless, concentrating only on problems may provide a distorted and incomplete assessment of the company's operations and personnel.

Chapter 18

Looking Deeper into the P&L

IN Chapter 17, using Exhibit 17.3, the composition of the various expenses of the sales department was used as an example to analyze why that department was operating over budget and consuming an increasing portion of revenue. Similar analyses should be done for the company's other departments on a quarterly basis. However, a departmental expense analysis is only one way to look at the costs and expenses picture.

A Different Perspective

Many of the expenses appearing on a departmental expense analysis presumably come under the direct control of that department's manager. Some expenses, such as rent, utility costs, and payroll fringes, will be allocated to a department on the basis of some formula. Even though a department may incur or be allocated an expense, the manager may not have responsibility for, control of, or authority over that expense. For example, casualty and liability insurance premium costs may be allocated among all departments, but only one manager, say the CFO, may be responsible for selecting the insurance carrier and negotiating the coverage and the rates. Thus, as valuable and informative as expense analyses are from a departmental perspective, they do not always provide management with a useful grasp of total costs and expenses by basic type or class of expenditure. A different type of summary must be prepared to provide that information, although the data necessary for that summary are easily obtained from the various departmental analyses.

Exhibit 18.1, prepared for the entire year, is a useful summary of

Exhibit 18.1

Hypothetical Technology Company
Comparison Of Actual And Budgeted Expenses - All Departments
By Quarters - For The Year 1988 - $,000 Omitted

	First Quarter Ending March 31							Second Quarter Ending June 30						
	<----------Actual-------->					Budget	Over	<----------Actual-------->					Budget	Over
	Mfg	R&D	Sales	G&A	Total	Total	(Und)	Mfg	R&D	Sales	G&A	Total	Total	(Und)
Wages and Salaries:														
Direct labor - assembly	190				190	165	25	188				188	175	13
Direct labor - machine shop	48				48	45	3	52				52	45	7
Departmental management	30	10	25	30	95	100	(5)	30	10	25	30	95	100	(5)
Supervision and foremen	48			14	62	60	2	48			14	62	60	2
Engineering	25	49			74	115	(41)	30	58			88	100	(12)
Field sales			42		42	35	7			49		49	42	7
Field service			36		36	30	6			42		42	36	6
Purchasing	22				22	12	10	23				23	22	1
Stockroom	33				33	30	3	36				36	33	3
Receiving and shipping	27				27	25	2	28				28	27	1
Quality control	21				21	20	1	23				23	20	3
Maintenance	15				15	12	3	17				17	15	2
Accounting				25	25	26	(1)				25	25	26	(1)
Clerical	31	5	9	18	63	60	3	33	5	9	18	65	63	2
EDP				9	9	9					9	9	9	
Total wages and salaries	490	64	112	96	762	744	18	508	73	125	96	802	773	29
Payroll Fringes:														
Health insurance premium	90	13	18	15	136	125	11	91	15	20	15	141	140	1
Life insurance premium	10	4	2	2	18	15	3	10	5	2	2	19	19	0
FICA taxes - employer's share	35	4	8	7	54	52	2	36	4	9	7	56	56	0
Overtime premium	3				3		3	5				5		5
Total payroll fringes	138	21	28	24	211	192	19	142	24	31	24	221	215	6
Other Departmental Expenses:														
Amortization - leasehold improvements	20	6			26	25	1	20	6			26	26	
Depreciation expense - machinery	36	6			42	40	2	46	6			52	42	10
Depreciation expense - autos			6		6	6				6		6	6	
Depreciation expense - office equip.	7	2	4	8	21	19	2	7	2	4	8	21	21	
Total depreciation & amortization	63	14	10	8	95	90	5	73	14	10	8	105	95	10
Rent	30	6	3	5	44	44		30	6	3	5	44	44	
Utilities costs	40	6	2	3	51	50	1	40	6	2	3	51	50	1
Telephone	8	3	10	4	25	24	1	8	3	10	4	25	24	1
Liability and casualty insurance	30	6	5	2	43	45	(2)	30	6	5	2	43	45	(2)
Repairs and maintenance	25	4	1	3	33	25	8	25	4	12	3	44	25	19
Operating supplies	38	6		1	45	35	10	38	6		1	45	35	10
Prototype materials		7			7	10	(3)		13			13	19	(6)
Advertising expense			53		53	50	3			60		60	30	30
Travel expense	2	1	58	1	62	31	31	1	1	54	1	57	45	12
Office supplies expense	21	6	3	1	31	30	1	12	6	3	3	24	30	(6)
Outside professional services		5		15	20	15	5		5		23	28	25	3
Miscellaneous expense	16	5	5	8	34	30	4	16	5	5	9	35	30	5
Total Other Departmental Expenses	273	69	150	51	543	479	64	273	75	164	62	574	497	77
Total All Departmental Expenses	901	154	290	171	1,516	1,415	101	923	172	320	182	1,597	1,485	112

	Third Quarter Ending September 30							Fourth Quarter Ending December 31							Total Actual For The Year
	<----------Actual-------->					Budget	Over	<----------Actual-------->					Budget	Over	
	Mfg	R&D	Sales	G&A	Total	Total	(Und)	Mfg	R&D	Sales	G&A	Total	Total	(Und)	Year
Wages and Salaries:															
Direct labor - assembly	195				195	200	(5)	188				188	175	13	761
Direct labor - machine shop	55				55	55		42				42	45	(3)	197
Departmental management	32	10	25	30	97	100	(3)	32	10	25	30	97	100	(3)	384
Supervision and foremen	50			19	69	65	4	50			19	69	70	(1)	262
Engineering	33	60			93	115	(22)	30	60			90	110	(20)	345
Field sales			56		56	49	7			56		56	49	7	203
Field service			48		48	42	6			54		54	42	12	180
Purchasing	23				23	25	(2)	20				20	20		88
Stockroom	37				37	40	(3)	36				36	40	(4)	142
Receiving and shipping	28				28	30	(2)	25				25	30	(5)	108
Quality control	23				23	23		23				23	23		90
Maintenance	17				17	17		17				17	17		66
Accounting				29	29	26	3				30	30	26	4	109
Clerical	34	5	9	20	68	65	3	33	5	12	20	70	65	5	266
EDP				13	13	9	4				15	15	15		46
Total wages and salaries	527	75	138	111	851	861	(10)	496	75	147	114	832	827	5	3,247
Payroll Fringes:															
Health insurance premium	95	15	22	18	150	150		92	15	24	18	149	149		576
Life insurance premium	12	5	3	3	23	20	3	11	5	3	3	22	22		82
FICA taxes - employer's share	37	5	10	7	59	57	2	35	5	10	10	60	60		229
Overtime premium								7				7		7	15
Total payroll fringes	144	25	35	28	232	227	5	145	25	37	31	238	231	7	902
Other Departmental Expenses:															
Amortization - leasehold improvements	20	6			26	26		20	6			26	26		104
Depreciation expense - machinery	46	9			55	57	(2)	53	9			62	57	5	211
Depreciation expense - autos			8		8	6	2			8		8	6	2	28
Depreciation expense - office equip.	7	2	5	10	24	21	3	7	2	5	10	24	21	3	90
Total depreciation & amortization	73	17	13	10	113	110	3	80	17	13	10	120	110	10	433
Rent	30	6	3	5	44	44		30	6	3	5	44	44		176
Utilities costs	42	6	2	3	53	50	3	40	6	2	3	51	50	1	206
Telephone	9	3	14	4	30	26	4	8	3	14	4	29	24	5	109
Liability and casualty insurance	32	6	5	2	45	45		30	6	5	2	43	45	(2)	174
Repairs and maintenance	30	2	2	3	37	35	2	26	4	2	2	34	35	(1)	148
Operating supplies	40	4		1	45	45		42	6		1	49	45	4	184
Prototype materials		18			18	20	(2)		20			20	19	1	58
Advertising expense			80		80	70	10			80		80	70	10	273
Travel expense	2	1	90	5	98	90	8	3	1	108	1	113	75	38	330
Office supplies expense	20	6	8	3	37	50	(13)	20	6	4	3	33	50	(17)	125
Outside professional services		5		35	40	30	10		5		45	50	35	15	138
Miscellaneous expense	24	8	13	18	63	47	16	20	7	9	9	45	50	(5)	177
Total Other Departmental Expenses	302	82	238	89	703	662	41	299	87	240	85	711	652	59	2,531
Total All Departmental Expenses	973	182	403	228	1,786	1,750	36	940	187	424	230	1,781	1,710	71	6,680

expenses that permits management to see, on one schedule, most of the expenses incurred by the company regardless of the department involved. Except for the top P&L statement, this is one of the few schedules in which important financial data are accumulated and presented from a companywide perspective. This schedule should be prepared each quarter, by quarter, and on a year-to-date basis so that you can more easily detect trends, seasonal variations, and growth in the various types of expenses.

The amount of detail shown is directly related to the number of accounts in the company's chart of accounts and how diligently the accounting personnel code the various invoices, bills, vouchers, and journals. If the chart of accounts is skimpy or the accounting clerks are not accurate, the data ultimately obtained will be meaningless. While a complete, detailed chart of accounts is a little more difficult to use, the quality and quantity of information will prove to be a worthwhile investment.

What You Don't Know Can Hurt the Company

In the summary analysis illustrated by Exhibit 18.1, expenses that in any one department may have seemed relatively small take on a larger significance when viewed from a companywide perspective. For example, noting that the company spent a total of $576,000 during the year for health insurance premiums may trigger a complete review of the principal providers of the entire employee benefits program; or that $266,000 of payroll being spent for nonspecific clerical work may justify a serious review of the paperwork system in the company.

Sometimes management may discover that significant amounts of money are routinely being spent in areas with little explanation or identification. Exhibit 18.1 tells us that $125,000 was spent on items under the heading "office supplies" and $177,000 was spent under the heading "miscellaneous expense." What are the various, bigger items that add up to that large total? Just how many items can be classified as "miscellaneous"?

It is possible that repeated expenditures for the same or similar expenses are being made that, in their aggregate, may warrant their own separate expense-account status. Suppose the company's bad-debt write-offs were routinely being charged to "miscellaneous expense" by the accounting department, or the costs of assembly or machine shop rework were being charged to "miscellaneous expense" by the manufacturing department. Using nonspecific or generic account titles as a catchall for a variety of small, miscellaneous expenditures is fine, but when the aggregate total of all expenditures charged to those accounts becomes significant, you must reexamine the composition of those "catchall" accounts. It may be time to create some new account classifications to segregate such expenses. You should never have to *guess* what kind of expenditure is included under any one category or classification, especially when large amounts are involved.

Analyzing the composition of a specific account can be a laborious task. Although the process may vary depending upon the complexity and sophistication of the accounting system, the accounting department usually must trace back all charges, as reflected in the journals, voucher register, or checkbook, made to the specific expense account in order to identify the vendors or sources. Then, accounting must examine the file of those vendors' paid bills. To facilitate this process and reduce the number of individual invoices that must be reviewed, minimum dollar limits are set below which no detailed analysis is necessary. As time-consuming as this process may seem, if your internal control processes are reliable, it should be required only when you no longer know the composition of the charges to an account, are surprised at the total being charged to an account, or are performing a periodic management review and audit of expenditures.

Chapter 19

Gross Profit Margin

ONE of the most underused but valuable bits of information readily available to management relates to the gross profit. Gross profit is the difference between the net sales dollars received and the cost of goods and/or services sold. For profitable operations, the gross profit must be more than the portion of sales revenue absorbed by all other company expenses.

The Forgotten Number on the P&L

Since most managers are sales-revenue and net-profit oriented, they tend to focus their attention on the top and bottom line of the operating statement; then, with a critical eye, they examine the various operating expenses (sales, marketing, engineering, general and administrative), giving only a scant glance to the company's gross profit. Perhaps one reason for this inattention is the complexity inherent in developing the gross profit number itself, especially in a multiproduct company. While it is presented as a simple subtraction of sales minus the costs of items sold, the number is actually the tip of an iceberg. In reality, the gross profit number is the accumulated result of perhaps thousands of individual sales of different products at different quantities and prices. Subtracted from these is the dollar impact of thousands of transactions involving inventory, material, labor, and factory and manufacturing overhead and expenses, all of which have been affected by matters as diverse as management decisions, the weather, and a fire at a supplier's warehouse. No wonder gross profit analysis is often ignored. When presented as a single number, it can be overwhelming.

Analyze and Learn

Since part of the gross profit equation is sales revenue, and management almost always pays close attention to incoming orders and their pricing, it is probably the cost-of-goods-sold portion of the equation that is the least understood. Even in a fairly modest manufacturing or distribution operation, many factors become part of the equation. Consider this simple example of a typical cost-of-goods-sold summary:

Beginning inventory		$10,000
+ Material purchases		5,500
+ Direct labor		3,300
+ Indirect labor		1,200
+ Factory overhead expenses		
Payroll fringe	$1,500	
Factory supplies	300	
Depreciation	200	
Utilities	100	2,100
Total goods available for sale		22,100
Less: Closing inventory		11,100
Cost of goods sold		$11,000

For all its simplicity, the cost-of-goods-sold statement is a melting pot for diverse data, and frequently it obscures significant facts and events that have had a serious impact on the company's performance. Unless more detail is derived through techniques such as standard costs, variance accounting, and marginal cost analysis, management will continue to see the forest but not be able to tell one tree from another. Even if each cost category had a budgeted amount with which it was to be compared, it would be meaningless if you didn't know such things as the actual product mix in the beginning inventory, the actual product mix manufactured, the actual product mix sold, and the actual product mix in the ending inventory. Does the cost-of-goods-sold statement tell you that $1,200 of inventory items produced last year was written off as obsolete this year, and can you determine the impact it had on the gross profit performance of the current period? The questions are endless, and unfortunately there are usually too few answers given. The first way out of this mess is to begin asking the right questions about your gross profit margin.

Must I Be Overrun with Accountants?

You need not be surrounded by accountants to have a sound grasp of what is happening and what has happened. In general, the better your accounting and management information systems, the better and more timely the data you and your management team should get. But even without a herd of accounting personnel, you can obtain sufficient details to use the gross profit calculation. To start, you must have a reasonably good idea of what the gross profit margin *should* be.

Concentrate on your more important products (from the standpoint of anticipated sales dollar volume) and do a detailed compilation of what each one's unit cost and average net selling price should be under conditions you anticipate will prevail during the coming period. Use whatever hard facts you do have or estimate and make educated guesses where necessary. This need not be an overwhelming task. No matter how many products you carry in your product line, more than likely only 20 percent of the product line will generate 80 percent of the sales dollar volume.

Having established what the bulk of the cost of goods sold should be, you can then do a similar, but more limited, construction of several other products selected from those of lesser volume importance. The aggregate of the two sets of information should approximate your estimate of the total, actual gross profit margin under the circumstances you have forecasted. If at the end of the period you find a significant difference between what you expected and what actually happened, then you must go back and find out why.

The definition of a significant difference will vary from company to company for many reasons, but a difference greater than 2 or 3 percent should be investigated: for example, predicted gross margin, 47 percent; actual gross margin, 45 percent. You should be able to predict your gross margin for a given period that closely, or else you should know why you will not hit the target *while the period is in progress.* If you miss the prediction by a significant, surprising amount, then you don't know what's going on in your own company, which is another problem entirely.

A Misguided Set of Values

It is not uncommon to find a management style that maintains tight control on salesmen's expense reports or on long-distance calls, yet places little or no value on a good cost-accounting system to track and report product costs on a real-time basis. Management may be unwilling to bear the costs of maintaining accurate perpetual inventory records, tracking ins and outs, with periodic test counting done on a regular basis. Such a management style, unless accompanied by a great deal of luck, is doomed to eventual failure, and the company will pay a heavy price.

Being able to control the gross profit margin is critical to the survival and success of every business. The gross profit margin is arguably the second most important number on the profit-and-loss statement. As it is the result of interaction between sales revenues (units sold x selling prices) and cost of goods sold (units made or purchased x costs), the gross margin lies directly on the critical path to net profit. It must not be neglected.

Why Are We Selling This?

One of the hidden benefits of gross profit analysis is that management may gain greater insight into the margin contribution of its individual products. Not every product will yield the same gross margin, and frequently some products don't make an appropriate profit contribution but have remained in the "catalog" for years. It's not that these products contribute *no* gross margin, but rather the effort required to keep that product in the line may be better served for some other product. Dropping products (and the sales revenue they produce) is a painful task for management and its sales force; the institutional and emotional resistance against doing so is usually formidable. Nevertheless, paring down the product line is a normal, routine step in intelligent business management.

An objective appraisal of *all* the direct and indirect costs of keeping a product alive may yield surprising results. Some products that on the surface may seem profitable may actually consume so much indirect support (installation, free service, advertising) that their bottom-line contribution may be negligible. Others may require enormous financial obligations (inventory commitments, extended credit terms to customers) that actually impair the business' ability to compete or expand in different, more rewarding product and market areas.

What Business Are We In Anyway?

Over time, a company may develop a damaging "multiple personality syndrome" if its product line contains too great a range of unit-price and gross-profit variations. This syndrome may affect how top management makes decisions and even on how the company is organized, often with serious negative side-effects on profitability and morale. Usually, management doesn't realize it is suffering until some extraordinary event or crisis occurs.

*

Rash & Obtuse Company manufactured precision equipment and supplies used by an important, growing segment of the electronics industry. The price range for its equipment was $30,000 to $80,000 per unit. Each piece of equipment sold also needed a separate replaceable tool as it operated. These high-precision tools sold for only $8.00 each and lasted, at best, only four hours. Over the course of a year of single-shift operation, one piece of equipment might require 700 to 1,000 tools per shift. The gross profit margin on a typical $50,000 model might be 45 percent, or $22,500, while the gross profit margin on the $8.00 tool might be 25 percent or $2.00. The company's annual equipment sales were $50 million, while their tool sales were $8 million.

The equipment products and the tool products each had separate division managers who reported to the company president. Since a customer would also need an ongoing supply of tools, both equipment and tool sales were handled by the same field sales personnel under a vice-president of sales reporting to the company president.

Given the significant difference in the prices and profit margins of the two product lines, Rash & Obtuse experienced several internal problems, some obvious and some not so obvious. The salesmen, with part of their compensation consisting of sales commission, usually wanted to spend most, if not all, of their selling time on the big-ticket equipment. Forced to use the company's field sales force, the tool division manager had to battle constantly for his division's share of salesmen's time and attention. The gross profit generated by tool sales didn't permit the tool division to have its own field sales force.

The narrow margin in the tools meant that pennies were important in controlling costs and manufacturing efficiency, whereas the equipment's gross margin permitted a more flexible approach to unit cost accounting, estimating, and manufacturing efficiency. Similar conflicts arose in negotiating price concessions and discounts to customers who ordered both equipment and tools. The company tended to treat the tools almost as a giveaway item, much to the consternation of the tool division manager. From a different perspective, the administrative demands placed on the tool division by the company's standard systems and procedures, which were designed to handle those of the larger, more complex equipment division, were out of proportion.

Ultimately, after going through three tool division managers, the company resolved most of its "multiple-personality" problems by granting the tool division greater independence. It was permitted to hire some direct sales personnel of its own and allowed to set up its own administrative and cost-accounting procedures. Every effort was made to allow the entrepreneurial spirit of the tool division's management to achieve its own destiny without playing second fiddle to the equipment group. In less than two years, the tool division was able to increase its sales volume, gross margins, and overall profit contribution.

While not every company may have such obvious gross-profit-margin differentials as Rash & Obtuse, many companies do have revenue-generating spare parts and/or service departments in which the economic and management factors are different from those in the main product divisions. If this is true for your company, you should take a close and careful look at the advantages and disadvantages that might accrue to the overall company operations if a greater degree of independence and freedom of action were granted to such departments or product lines.

Chapter 20

Product Mix

THIS bit of financial advice sounds simple, perhaps even simplistic: Target your maximum selling effort on the products that generate the highest gross profit margin. You'll fatten your company's operating results with no technology risk and no additional capital investment. All it takes to make a big difference at the bottom line is some shrewd analysis and the right incentive plan. If this sounds like a basic technique for managing profits, you're right. But it's surprising how frequently managements overlook the basics.

Consider this: Do you get a regular report reflecting the gross profit margin of each product or service you sell? Besides pounding your desk about high manufacturing costs, do you use profit analysis to target sales-incentive plans and product-advertising or promotion programs that push high-margin items? If not, you're missing out on a vital, although basic, management tool.

It's Not the Price

In almost every business, each product or service sold yields widely different margins that frequently have little to do with the selling price. Often big-ticket items contribute the lowest gross margins in the entire product line. Yet, most commission or incentive plans aim primarily—or exclusively—at improving total sales volume, instead of serving to stimulate sales of the most *profitable* products. If they do hike sales of the most profitable items, it's usually by accident. So, sales volume goes up, the salesmen make more money—and the company's profit rate goes down.

There are three reasons why this happens:

1. The typical package of accounting data supplied to top management doesn't reflect up-to-date gross profit margin by product. Even worse, the sales and marketing managers have no idea of the gross margin mix. At best, only the gross profit earned on total sales is reported to the various management groups, without a breakdown by product.

2. Most sales or marketing managers are measured and rewarded on sales growth, with the company's profit improvement only a secondary consideration. Salesmen are usually paid a commission on individual or territorial sales volume, so they concentrate on products that are easiest to sell. The result? Executives with the primary responsibility to design and implement an incentive plan have neither the data nor the inclination to consider profit improvement as a primary goal.

3. When sales volume increases and total profits are up, top management is often blind to the fact that the margin of profit earned on sales has decreased. In their joy over an increase in the bottom line, they often overlook a deterioration in the gross profit margin. Routinely accepting that situation discloses a management blind spot and a missed opportunity to have done even better.

A Better Way

What should you do? Analyze the gross-margin contribution of your various products, then use targeted promotion programs to stimulate the sales of those products with the highest margin.

You must start by analyzing the gross profit and margin contribution of the present product mix. This doesn't have to be a huge task if you remember the "20 percent:80 percent" rule:

> Usually, 20 percent of a company's products sold generate 80 percent of its sales volume.
> So, restrict your study to those products, plus any new products that aren't yet in the top 20 percent but that could be important in the future.

Make certain to consider any extra expenses routinely incurred in the sale of a product that are not reflected in the normal analysis of the cost of goods sold. For example, a product with what initially appears to be a high gross profit margin may require more company-paid installation or warranty service and is not the profit-generator it seems to be. Such factors must be considered when the product-cost data are accumulated and used in your analysis.

In Exhibit 20.1, sales volume totals $1,050,000 and is derived from the sale of 700 units each of products A, B, and C, plus 1,500 units of other assorted products. The total gross profit is $458,500. Based upon the current product mix, the weighted average gross profit margin for all the products is 43.67 percent. Product B, at 60 percent, has the largest rate of gross profit margin of all the products sold.

Now suppose you offer the sales force an extra incentive bonus of $12 for every unit of Product B sold. Exhibit 20.2 reflects what happens if a total of 3,600 units of all products is sold, the same as in the previous period. However, the product mix changes when the sales force responds to the bonus stimulation.

Exhibit 20.1

Product	*Dollar Sales*	*Quantity Sold*	*Price*	*Cost*	*Gross Profit*	*Total Profit Contribution*	*Profit Margin*
A	$ 420,000	700	$600	$420	$180	$126,000	30%
B	280,000	700	400	160	240	168,000	60%
C	140,000	700	200	100	100	70,000	50%
Others	210,000	1500	(—	*Varies*	—)	94,500	45%
Total	$1,050,000	3600				$458,500	43.67%

Exhibit 20.2

Product	*Dollar Sales*	*Quantity Sold*	*Price*	*Cost*	*Gross Profit*	*Total Profit Contribution*	*Profit Margin*
A	$ 300,000	500	$600	$420	$180	$ 90,000	30%
B	440,000	1100	400	160	240	264,000	60%
C	100,000	500	200	100	100	50,000	50%
Others	210,000	1500	(—	*Varies*	—)	94,500	45%
Total	$1,050,000	3600				$498,500	47.48%

By stimulating an increased selling effort of the product with the highest rate of gross profit margin, sales of Product B went up 400 units. Even though sales of Products A and C went down by 200 units each, total gross profit went to $498,500—a gain of $40,000—and increased the weighted-average gross-profit percentage to 47.48 percent.

After you deduct $13,200 in bonuses paid to the sales force for 1,100 units of Product B sold, the bottom line reveals that you are $26,800 ahead—a significant improvement from the results in the prior period.

ALL IN THE MIX

Actively managing a company's product mix through deployment of its selling resources is a critical factor in the struggle to maximize business profits. Although many companies spend heavily for sales and marketing activities to create a powerful sales effort, that force is frequently misdirected.

Analyzing the gross profit margin of each product will highlight those with the potential to provide an extra boost to profits if given a sales push through a targeted plan.

Whether developing an incentive program for the sales department, deciding which products to advertise, or employing other company sales tools, the profit-oriented manager will aim for an improvement in the total gross profit margin and not just an increase in overall sales volume.

Chapter 21

Quality, a Rediscovered Management Task

WITHIN the last few decades, the problem of product and service quality has gained the attention of American business managers in a wide variety of industries. Unfortunately, this "discovery" was somewhat belated when compared to the actions of the buying public. And it was even later that business managers realized that internal emphasis on quality required more than an interoffice memo and a slogan. It needed top management attention, a corporatewide commitment, and constant reinforcement. Where once most of the internal concerns regarding quality were the exclusive (and easily ignored) province of a few introverted engineers buried deep in the manufacturing department, quality now demands the attention and active participation of all the senior executives of the company.

Even if not driven by more altruistic forces, businesses have found it to be in their own self-interest to deal with the issue of quality. For one thing, product liability risks have become a major concern of all segments of the business community, including the product manufacturer, the component suppliers, the wholesalers and retailers, plus local, state, and federal governments. In fact, without a valid quality-assurance and control system in-house, it may be almost impossible for a company to purchase product liability insurance.

In the marketplace, the buying public, including industrial buyers, are more sophisticated and discerning regarding the issue of quality. Certainly price is always a consideration in the buying decision, but in terms of product performance, reliability, and expectations, more and more people want to make certain "they're getting what they paid for, and then some." Failure to measure up is an easy way for any company, whether manufacturer, service organization, or retailer, to lose sales and market share.

Another factor to contend with is the wide publicity given to lapses in quality and reliability. Several consumer-oriented magazines enjoy immense popularity and circulation, providing reviews and ratings on a variety of products and services. Local and network TV stations are quick to publicize quality and reliability breakdowns, product recalls, shams and scams. Given the "dog-eat-dog" competition at the retail level, now significantly in the hands of a handful of powerful, mega-retail organizations, most retailers won't stand for too many complaints regarding a product before they drop it from their shelves. For the smaller, more local businesses, "word-of-mouth" is a double-edged sword: Make a customer happy and he may tell a few friends; disappoint him and you can count on his telling everyone who will listen.

Quality Can Be Profitable

The first and perhaps most essential lesson management can learn is that giving proper attention to quality considerations can make money for the company over the longer term. Regardless of the price level of the products being manufactured and sold, maintaining a program of quality assurance and control consistent with the price/market niche targeted by the company can enhance profitability, and quite possibly, sales volume as well.

Unfortunately, most traditional accounting systems and reports are not designed to highlight the impact of quality (or the lack of it) in the profit-and-loss statement or supporting schedules. Frequently it is impossible to tell how much poor quality is costing the company in hard dollars and cents. Complaints from customers and sales personnel, lost orders, and returned products are fairly obvious results of letting quality slip. Not so obvious are the many rework hours buried in the labor-time reports, poor procurement practices, excessive manufacturing hours resulting from filing and hand-fitting parts, rejects piling up at the final assembly floor, the assembly foreman with caches of good components hidden in his desk drawers "just in case," the field service department working overtime. You can be sure the hidden costs of poor quality are scattered throughout the company, where they remain masked by the normal, business-as-usual routine. So, while your newfound enthusiasm for quality is gaining momentum, make certain you give adequate consideration to the improvements needed in the cost accounting and performance measurement systems.

It is primarily through the accounting system that you will discover the hard facts concerning how much money you can save, and will earn, through an effective quality program. Frequently, a special task force of personnel from accounting, quality, and manufacturing will be able to develop new, more informative reports that can serve as a strong incentive to implement a sound quality-assurance and control program. Remember, measuring product or service quality using instruments, statistical methods, life-tests, and surveys is *not* the same as measuring dollars and cents.

Compromising Quality

No matter how noble-sounding and idealistic, quality is still a trade-off—a balance between considerations of cost, reliability, and time—and it is vital that top management understand and establish that balance correctly. For example, consider the balancing act regarding those three issues faced by NASA's managers in the space program. Given the realities of safety, budget constraints, and the timing of launch windows dictated solely by the laws of physics, it is quite a challenge. What about the manufacturer of economy cars. How many coats of paint will the cost structure permit on his cars compared to the multiple, hand-rubbed finishes put on luxury cars? How tight should the doors, hood, and trunk lid fit before a car is "OK to ship"? How much component reliability and quality can one really afford to put into a line of can openers and juice squeezers when those products are just another "me too" item sold in the highly competitive, discount store market? How often have you spent hundreds for a product only to have it fail because of a knob or button that cost less than a dollar?

The truth is, given the selling-price constraints set by the market for any product, regardless of its quality level, seeking affordable improvements in procedures, processes, and practices will enhance both product quality and its bottom-line profit contribution. The challenge for managers of manufacturing or service organizations is to be able to assess intelligently the technical and business considerations involved in the trade-offs before leaping to conclusions. There are no easy paths or shortcuts to upgrading product and service quality—just patience, hard work, and the dedicated input and participation of practically *every* employee of the company.

A Systems Approach

As with most activities in a business, improving the quality of products and service a company provides requires a systems approach. In his book, *Quality Assurance in Service Organizations*, Anthony DiPrimio describes the effort, which he calls a "Quality Assurance & Service Reliability Program," as a "planned, systematic way of finding and eliminating the root causes of quality problems." DiPrimio breaks the program into four essential components:

1. Quality measures: Determining the level of quality in order to evaluate the problem and provide a basis for monitoring it on an ongoing basis. How will quality be defined and measured? What measures are already in place and are they meaningful?
2. Quality engineering: The process of deciding how, when, and where quality will be measured. This includes data collection, analysis, and reporting. All measurements must be fair, accurate, and consistent.
3. Quality education: Taking the time to explain the program's concept, how it will operate, and what it will mean to the employees and the company. In addition, new skills, methods, and procedures may need to be taught to both the blue-collar and white-collar work forces. It is virtually impossible to overestimate the importance of this education component in order to achieve and maintain any significant success.
4. Management of input: In order to hold a work area responsible for the quality of its output, the quality of the material it receives to work on must be monitored. Thus, in a manufacturing organization, the quality of the original product design, tools, equipment, and the raw materials and components purchased will have an overwhelming impact on the performance of any work group. Similarly, the performance of service organizations is also affected by the quality of the data sent to it from outside the organization.

Begin at the Beginning

For a manufacturer, quality considerations depend upon a few seemingly simple but enormously complex undertakings. The first is the design of the product, the components selected, and the various manufacturing processes used to put it together. Each of these elements affects the quality and reliability of the end-product. It's a package deal: Screw up on just one of them and you will end up with a product below your anticipated quality level no matter what you do later on.

You must establish clearly defined and agreed-upon product specifications, including cost, selling price, and performance targets when you either develop a new product or improve an established product. These targets must be reviewed, tested, and revalidated, as work on the design proceeds. If you must compromise or make adjustments, make sure you understand any risks that might be involved.

Next in the critical path are the employees, and this means *all* employees, from the factory workers, the foreman, and supervisors, to all levels of management above. If your employees are not active, motivated participants in the program, then it won't matter how clever and elegant the product design is or how carefully chosen the components were. Gaining the support of the employees is no easy task. Yes, it requires constant education and reinforcement; yes, it requires seeking out and listening to employee input and suggestions; yes, most employees would rather do things right than wrong; but it also requires some "glue" to make that all happen and hang together. That "glue" is called *incentive*—a reason for the employees to want to improve quality.

Giving a Little to Get a Little

Your employees must be tangibly rewarded for improving quality. Either through a bonus plan or profit-sharing plan, they must reap some of the benefits of having made their own commitment to quality. Individual recognition, honors, awards, and badges are nice frills and should be part of the total program, but the dollar speaks the loudest and goes further. As the program begins to produce results, those results must be translated into a monetary award for the employees, and the rewards must continue so long as the quality objectives are being met.

There are some risks in giving monetary rewards, especially if they are restricted to just a few large amounts. Obviously someone may feel cheated and overlooked. It's far better to spread a fair share of the awards among as many employees as possible, even if a handful of the undeserving also get a share. If the size of the awards seems insignificant, either you haven't correctly figured out how much the quality program is now saving you (or what the old ways were costing you), or you are retaining too large a share for the company.

Across-the-Board Quality

It is almost automatic to consider matters regarding quality only in association with customers. But that is not the entire picture. Other activities within a company, whether manufacturing or service, need attention in terms of the quality aspect and may have nothing directly to do with customers. The completeness of data transferred from one department to another, how promptly information is transmitted, how well records, drawings, and blueprints are done, the communications systems, interoffice mail service, message centers, filing systems—in short, the quality of every administrative function within the company might be reviewed and improved. One of management's objectives should be to institutionalize the concept of quality in everything the company does. Becoming sensitive to quality and making it an integral part of the corporate culture and focus will benefit not only your customers but your entire staff as well.

PART 4

The External Environment

ALL companies contend with outside influences, including customers, competitors, vendors, and the local, national—even international—economic climate. Because most of these factors operate beyond your direct control, often on an adversarial basis, you must recognize both the dangers and the opportunities they present. The more you understand their "hows and whys," the greater your chances for success. It may be relatively easy for managers to use their authority to manage within their companies, but special skills, awareness and experience are needed to cope with the external environment. Your knowledge, self-confidence, and reactions will have significant impact on the survival and future welfare of your company.

Chapter 22

Marketing and Sales

ONE major defect of many companies, even those with a fair degree of business success, is a lack of solid, in-depth knowledge of the markets and the customers within each market they seek to sell. Certainly the sales personnel may know the names of the purchasing agents, managers, and engineers who sign the requisitions and purchase orders, but the reasons how and why the decisions to buy are made, or why a company selects a specific supplier's product over others offered just aren't known, and no effort is made to learn. Decision-making by buyers is more than the obvious price-delivery-quality factors, and any management that restricts its thinking to those three factors alone is probably losing market share.

Market Intelligence

No matter what your business, you must continuously analyze the various factors in the market environment you will be addressing. How else can you develop and adjust your marketing plan? Each market and each customer within a market has its own needs, wants, and problems. Too many companies are blind when it comes to knowing who and/or what are the buying influencers in the mechanics of the purchase decision. For example, it may be a purchasing agent that issues the first order to buy 500 reams of a certain brand of copy-machine paper, but you can be sure that the supervisor of the duplicating department (the one who had to constantly unjam all the machines) will have something to say about who gets the next order. A company choosing a computer system may place more importance on how many office terminals can have simultaneous access to the system than on the total system price.

A salesman may proudly boast that his centerless grinders have a "mean time between failure" of 10,000 hours, but a prospective customer may be more interested in getting a unit delivered within ten days and couldn't care less if the unit shouldn't need a service call for three years.

The reasons behind "what is purchased and from whom the purchase is made" may be unclear, but they must be addressed specifically by any seller who hopes to compete successfully. The seller and the sales and marketing personnel must take the time and make the effort to know their product and their competitors', the general market, and the different customers within the market.

Many retail organizations whose sales personnel regularly deal with consumers on a one-on-one basis, have developed highly efficient methods for making the sale. Often these tactics are—or border on—illegal. They include high pressure and bait and switch, but they produce the desired result—a sale. Such sales personnel have been taught the right "buttons" to push with each customer. They have been schooled on the objections and questions that will be raised and how to respond. Obviously, a business should not resort to illegal or unsavory tactics to sell its products, but the principle of training your sales force *how to sell* is valid. Every sales person should be trained to read and understand the selling situation at any customer he or she encounters. The correct answers, how to handle objections, how to ask for and close the order, should become second nature to the sales force.

Pin the Tail on the Donkey

A lack of market intelligence is not uncommon in retail organizations, and many retailers remain blind to the realities of their specific market. Some succeed at least marginally, in spite of themselves, because of location. In this obvious example, assume you are a pharmacist seeking to open a new store somewhere in a growing suburban area. Should you just close your eyes and choose the location by sticking a pin in a map? Of course not. You would do current and projected studies of the area's population demographics, perhaps also using that data to make some initial inventory/stocking/pricing decisions. You would study auto and pedestrian traffic patterns, local competition, and any number of other factors, knowing that once you signed that five- or ten-year lease, you would be locked into that location. Sounds pretty simple and straightforward, but that may not be sufficient. Suppose you were able to get space in a new neighborhood shopping center?

Since most shopping centers permit only one drugstore in the center, that store will have a relatively captive market for medical prescriptions. A few doors away, however, the giant food market, open 24 hours a day, has aisle space dedicated to many of the same nonprescription (toothpaste, brushes, hair spray, aspirin, mouth wash) items the drugstore is hoping to sell. The food market may generate a lot of shopping center traffic, but how many come into the drugstore, and why? What about the people that don't come in? How can the drug store attract them and compete successfully? The owner's only chance is to implement a plan that convinces the neighborhood shoppers to buy nonprescription items from him. To do this he must understand his customers and learn the various factors that influence their buying decisions.

Intelligent marketing requires market intelligence, and this applies to big companies and small. However, market intelligence is not a one-shot affair; it is an ongoing process requiring review, revalidation, and revision. The danger to be avoided is that of looking inward. The source of market intelligence is *outside* the company, which means focusing on the needs and concerns of your customers.

A Real Sales Effort or Misguided Energy?

Imagine your company spending months to develop an expensive advertising and promotion campaign. Big bucks are spent to stock up on certain products at a favorable cost in anticipation of stimulating customer interest and demand for those products. The sales personnel have received instructions from management to get ready for the big push. A few weeks or months later, management wrings its hands in despair when the numbers come in. Yes, sales are up a little, but considerably less than expected in the targeted products. Why? Probably because everyone was being stimulated to act in a certain manner except your sale force.

One of the most frustrating sights for management is to see salesmen bringing in orders for products that are still under development in engineering. In most markets, customers are always looking for the latest technology, and an honest salesman will admit that it's easier to sell "new stuff" than the old products. Unless forced to do otherwise, it is reasonable to anticipate that the salesman will follow the path of least sales resistance.

The primary responsibility—or blame—for such situations usually rests with management and not the sales force. What is missing are the management controls and special incentives designed to shape the behavior and efforts of your sales force, and thereby your customers, to your advantage.

Order Takers and Order Getters Both Eat Carrots

Most of the time, salesmen are order takers. In fact, the bulk of your sales is probably the result of sales made regularly to the same or similar customers. On the other hand, order getters seek out new prospects and open new accounts. Both the order taker and order getter exist in most companies. Regardless of the composition of your company's sales force, both types can be trained and motivated to sell what it is that company management wants them to sell. At the heart of any motivation program is an incentive plan.

For many companies, a sales quota/commission system is the primary and probably the only tool management uses for motivating its sales force. The use of a "carrot" as an incentive is an old, time-proven technique that can produce positive results, *if* management knows how it should be developed, structured, and implemented. Unfortunately, too many companies fail to develop their "carrot" program.

The ineffective "carrot" is a sales quota program conceived in secrecy, mandated into effect without adequate communication, rigidly enforced, and then mysteriously abandoned when it doesn't work. It is one of the most destructive creations of management. Even worse, companies where sales quota programs are developed and implemented that way usually have another "bad" plan ready to go when the old one fails, as it inevitably will.

The symptom: a confused and unhappy sales force, unsure of its objectives, performing significantly below its potential, and experiencing high turnover. Incoming orders are not necessarily of the products hoped for or targeted by management. Meanwhile, time passes and top management is wringing its hands in despair.

A Checklist for Guidance

Successful sales quota programs have certain universal characteristics. If you follow the basic fundamentals, you can develop a program that will be beneficial to both the company and its sales organization:

1. Every sales quota should be attainable under normally antici-

pated conditions and with reasonable effort. If the quotas are set unrealistically high and are virtually impossible to accomplish, they will demotivate the sales personnel, just the opposite of what you are trying to accomplish.

2. The sales force should be asked for their input and suggestions during the conception phase of the program. By taking the time to consult with the salespeople beforehand, there is a better chance the program will be favorably received by the majority of the sales staff.

3. If the program is complicated in structure, computation, or measurement, it will create suspicion and mistrust. The more difficult it is to explain to the salespeople, the quicker they will be turned off by it.

4. A salesperson should get some form of reward for reaching or exceeding the quota. A program is not complete if it does not provide a tangible incentive for the participants. The relationship between so-called "base pay" and any amounts earned through the quota program must be integrated into an overall compensation plan for sales personnel.

5. The sales force and the company must be able to measure and report on their interim progress regularly and with relative ease. If one or both parties cannot tell how they are making out on the program, they will be unable to take any necessary corrective action until it is too late.

6. The time period covered by a sales quota should not be too long. Four separate quarterly quotas are better than one annual quota. Quotas developed for the shorter term tend to be more accurate in reflecting market realities and establishing valid objectives. In addition, more frequent goal-setting permits a salesperson, who might otherwise become discouraged by falling behind, to rekindle his efforts with a new "reachable" target and a chance to start fresh.

7. The program must have a logical purpose and premise, and the company must have clearly defined the goals it hopes to achieve through the program. If it doesn't make good business sense for the company, the program will not get the support of the sales force.

8. If conditions (the economy, products, prices, competitive factors) change, the program should be capable of some adjustment without being totally abandoned. Providing a reasonable amount of flexibility beforehand may avoid having to start the entire process over again.

Why All the Trouble?

The company's sales force represents a substantial investment in time and money. Management's responsibility is to use that force effectively to achieve the company's goals. For a sales quota program to be a productive management technique, it must motivate, communicate, guide, measure, and reward. And it must be fair. Successful programs require intelligent planning and preparation. They cannot be whipped up at the last minute and thrust upon the sales organization. When properly conceived, implemented, and managed, a sales quota program can yield excellent results through an improvement in sales, profits, and morale.

Important as a good sales quota program may be, it is just one segment of an overall sales and marketing strategy. No quota system makes up for the failure of a company to understand and define its market, intelligently position its products within that market, price its products correctly for the market, reach the market through effective advertising and distribution methods, and recruit and train qualified sales personnel.

Sales quotas can be a blunt instrument to bludgeon a sales force, but are a useful tool when applied with skill and purpose.

Chapter 23

Rediscovering the Customer

IN recent years, the perceived superior quality of imported Japanese and German products has seriously affected the prosperity, if not the continued survival, of many well-known American companies making competitive products. In other cases, the sometimes surly attitude of retail sales or service personnel has made would-be customers take their business elsewhere. These problems exist throughout the entire spectrum of industrial, wholesale, and retail businesses in America. Who is to blame? Certainly not the consumer. American business management bears the lion's share of the responsibility for the deterioration of American product quality and customer service. As normal business practices, shortsightedness, expediency, and grabbing the fast buck have a price, and that price is the loss of customer loyalty, respect, and continued patronage.

Lee Iacocca, the respected leader of Chrysler, embarked on an expensive national advertising campaign based on the fundamental principle of a "customer's bill of rights." Consider how revolutionary this is as a business concept—recognizing that people and companies who purchase the various products and services made and offered for sale are actually entitled to receive appropriate and commensurate value. Are American business enterprises finally waking up? Is it possible that Mr. Iacocca may have rediscovered a forgotten, but vital, basic business reality: that when you get right down to it, the customers will decide which businesses will succeed or fail? Equally as important, isn't it a concept that should be embraced and implemented by all profit-oriented business organizations, including yours?

Where Do You Buy?

When we or our company are consumers, more than likely we would like to believe in the motto "The customer is always right." Unfortunately, our experiences have taught us the wisdom of another motto, "Let the buyer beware." If you examine your own buying habits, you will discover that you make your purchases from business enterprises where you know you can expect honest product quality, good service, and timely delivery, all at a reasonable price and without a big hassle. If that is how you determine how and where you buy, why would you expect anyone else, including those to whom you try to sell, to expect less or act differently? Buyers are becoming more sophisticated and increasingly aware of quality and service in addition to price. If you want to retain and then build up your company's market share, why don't you make certain your company treats its customer contact and relationships in a manner that you, as a typical buyer, would find acceptable and attractive. It makes good business sense.

I'll Never Buy There Again

Every one of us has experienced the anger and frustration of spending good money and ending up with damaged, inferior, or misrepresented merchandise. To add insult to injury, when we've taken the trouble to complain, we've frequently been met with lies, hostility, and denials, or, if we've been lucky, a grudgingly-given replacement or refund. The result: That business has lost our patronage.

Certainly mistakes can happen. A product can have a defect or be damaged. Sometimes nothing is wrong with the product, but the customer is dissatisfied for some other reason. Be that as it may, the problem is: How does the business and the company representative in direct contact with the customer react? You must establish the standards of behavior expected from representatives of your company.

Get a Clear Picture

It is foolish for any manager to assume his company is exempt from quality or service problems. You will certainly have some. The questions are, How many? How bad? Where? and Why? You will need adequate data on the size and nature of the problems before you can take appropriate corrective action. First, you must obtain an objective assessment of how your company stacks up in customer service and product quality. If you're a large company with room in the budget, you can hire outside consultants to do public-opinion surveys, after-sale followup calls, comparison shopping, and other tests to ascertain your company's image vis-à-vis your customers. There are also cheaper, less scientific, but almost equally as informative steps you can take. Here are a few examples of things that can be done by even the smallest company:

1. Monitor amounts charged to warranty expenses in the P&L report carefully, and every few weeks review the details of all warranty claims submitted to the company. This will give you an idea of what is going wrong.
2. Ask friends or relatives to call your company to request information on products, such as pricing, delivery, or some technical information. Find out whether their calls were answered promptly and courteously, if they received accurate information, and what their general impressions of the company are based on that phone interchange. Also have them shop at your store or visit your offices or factory to see how they are treated by the sales, service, or other company personnel.
3. At random, call or write customers yourself to find out how they feel about your company and its products and services.

Whether your company is big or small, it is important that you continue ongoing examinations of how things look from the other side—the customer's perspective.

An Organizational Perspective

As manager of your company, you remain totally and fully responsible for the products it sells, the services it provides, and the manner in which customers are treated both before and after the sale. This is not a responsibility you can avoid or completely delegate away. At best, you can share it with other executives and make them jointly responsible along with you.

One enlightened response by business management to matters affecting its own best interests has been the recognition of the importance of internal quality control and/or quality assurance activities. Executives responsible for quality have been given greater clout and have been elevated to the inner corporate sanctum, reporting directly to the company president. By allowing direct communication with the president, many of the problems previously suppressed or ignored (when the quality organization reported to a lower-level executive responsible for manufacturing or engineering) now get full disclosure.

In addition, recognizing that quality must be designed into a product at its creation rather than trying to "inspect it in" afterward has given the manufacturing and engineering functions an entirely new attitude regarding their role and responsibilities. While many companies have made significant progress in the area of product quality and performance, much still remains to be done, perhaps especially the behavior of the sales and service personnel who are in direct contact with the customer. To remain competitive, you must get on the bandwagon and institute similar policies and practices in your company.

Taking Positive Action

Running TV commercials to convince the public that your company believes "the customer is always right" may be nothing more than expensive propaganda if you haven't also taken the appropriate steps to follow through on that promise. Realistically, a portion of the company's resources—time, money, and talent—must be dedicated to an ongoing in-house education program that reaches every level of the organization. The education program must describe clearly the manner in which the company and its employees should conduct themselves vis-à-vis its customers. It must also serve to institutionalize such behavior—that is, consistently demonstrate that the company will actually reward good behavior and rebuke bad behavior.

As with most company education programs, it must start at the top of the organization. If top management and the executives pay lip service to improving product quality, customer relations, and public confidence, no employee will take the program seriously. The key to making an educational program take root and produce positive results is to make certain employees understand it is in their self-interest—job security, raises, promotions—to learn and apply the instructions on an everyday basis.

Naturally, reasonable limits and guidelines must be established to assist employees in dealing with customer-service matters. If the management and application of those rules and guidelines are too strict, the entire program will fail. Customers will remain dissatisfied and the company will lose sales and profits.

One More Time for Basics

The success of every seller depends on the action of buyers. What your company does to attract, retain, or discourage buyers is under your control. Having magnificent showroom facilities, grandiose trade show exhibits, or amusing TV commercials means nothing in the long run if the buyers or would-be buyers think your product or service is of poor quality or overpriced, if their phone calls are not answered promptly and courteously, or if they are poorly treated by sales personnel. It is infinitely more difficult and expensive for any company to attempt to recapture customer goodwill that has been lost than to maintain that goodwill in the first place.

Chapter 24

The Outside Professionals

SOONER or later, every businessman must seek out certain professional services, such as a lawyer or certified public accountant, to support business operations. Within each profession there are specialties, such as taxes (federal, state, and local), corporate law, SEC law, SEC accounting, public liability law, or pension accounting. Not all legal or accounting firms (big or small) have the necessary experience and expertise in every area. But, with few exceptions, most lawyers or CPAs have the same thing in common: They think they know your business better than you do. For the privilege of paying their high fees, you can have them gladly tell you what is right (not much) and wrong (you need a lot of help) and how your business should be run.

Is There Honor among Thieves?

For the most part, lawyers and accountants are lousy businessmen. Few have faced the day-to-day problems of meeting a payroll, managing manufacturing, planning inventory, directing a marketing program, or the other myriad responsibilities faced daily in running a business. They may have had peripheral, arms-length contact with successful and unsuccessful companies and, to that end, may be able to provide some insight about the problems they have seen with other clients. That insight may be of value to you, but it is neither infallible nor absolute. Each business environment is different and conditions vary from company to company.

Frequently, a lawyer or accountant spends most of his or her time telling you why you shouldn't do what you want to do. Rather than assisting you in overcoming obstacles in your path, he may toss in a few more for you to contend with. Rare is the lawyer who says, "Sure you can, here's how," instead of "You can't because . . ." There is a simple economic reason for this: Invoice totals for professional fees are directly proportional to the frequency of "You can't because . . ." pronouncements.

In most business deals or activities where a lawyer must be consulted, there is usually another lawyer or some sort of "mindless institutional bureaucracy" involved on the other side. The businessman then becomes the "fee-paying" audience to the ritual dance of legal mumbo-jumbo played out to the bitter end.

What is a businessman to do in today's "I'll sue" society? Perhaps the best answer is to stay in control of the situation. Don't permit your company's needs to play second fiddle to what is essentially one of your hirelings. Use professionals if you must, but insist on prompt, complete, and capable performance of their responsibilities and assignments. Set time and budget limits with them, and make it clear you expect them to be met. Pay for results, accomplishment of objectives, and professional competence; don't pay for delays and excuses. There are many law firms and accounting organizations anxious to earn their fees from you and your company. You don't have to settle for mediocre performance. No one hands you a blank check in your business, so don't ever be anxious to give one out.

Consultants: The Here-Today, Gone-Tomorrow Experts

The ancient Chinese rulers made frequent use of consultants. The consultant was asked for advice and counsel and was handsomely rewarded if he proved to be correct. However, if proven incorrect, or if the advice resulted in failure, the wise ruler had the consultant beheaded. Obviously this made for a small but capable cadre of consultants.

Bringing in a consultant is a sure way of disrupting an organization's status quo. It's not that the consultant will impart any particular wisdom or offer problem-solving abilities; rather, it's because he or she will probably generate fear throughout the various levels of the company. This fear, whether well deserved or irrational, is something you must anticipate and prepare for in order to avoid a severe disruption in your company's operations.

You can be certain that the executives with the areas of expertise closest to that of the consultant's will feel threatened. If "shaking up the troops" is what you intend, fine. If, however, you want your management team to make the most effective use of what the consultant can contribute, then you absolutely must pave the way.

Most of your reasons for bringing in a consultant must be made known to and shared with your management team in advance. If possible, even the decision to bring in a consultant should be a joint one. The problems requiring a consultant must be recognized and defined. Bringing in a consultant for a witch-hunt can be disastrous to company morale and performance. Not only will the organization become chaotic, but the consultant's effectiveness will be impaired because he or she will receive little cooperation. The cost of the consultant will go up and the end results will be disappointing.

The Guys with the Briefcases Are Here

The consultant's end product or service must be defined in detail before any work is begun. Both you and the consultant must clearly understand and agree upon what is to be delivered, in what format, by when, and how much it will cost. All too often management is left with a fairly standard set of generalized recommendations or comments that would be similar for most companies, with little detailed information on how you can develop and implement whatever corrective actions are necessary.

Once the consultant begins work, you must insist upon regular meetings. You and your management team should periodically review what the consultant has done, as well as how and why he did it. Most of the reasons for taking your time to do this are obvious, but one may not be: Your company may learn some of the techniques used by the consultants for problem identification, analyses, and solving, which you can then apply in other areas on your own.

The Board of Directors: Rubber Stamp or Valuable Resource?

Too many business owners and managers are paranoid about having a board of directors whose members possess broad business experience, know-how, and independence. Instead, they choose a few of their relatives and the company's lawyer. Directors' meetings, if held, are annual perfunctory affairs confined to reelecting the same officers, authorizing a new check-signer or two, and rubber-stamping whatever the lawyer or the president put in front of them.

A properly constituted board of directors can be one of the most valuable resources a company owner or manager can have. You should seek out individuals whose experience and knowledge make them capable of making positive contributions to the management of the company, including the directions taken by the company and the formulation of its policies. But it takes more than just assembling such a board. You must then use the expertise of the board to your company's advantage.

You should hold regular and frequent meetings of the board, at least once a quarter. Discuss your business problems with them, explain the why's and wherefore's of any major management decisions taken since the last meeting, provide complete and accurate financial information to them, and, above all, listen. If you have chosen the members wisely, you will get back honest answers, good and useful advice, and a different perspective on the company and its problems. You should expect to pay the board members fair compensation for attending board meetings and any committee meetings.

Thanks, but No Thanks

When someone joins a board of directors, he or she becomes legally liable for a wide variety of company actions or inactions. Even with the purchase of "officers and directors liability insurance," it may be difficult for the smaller company to obtain qualified persons willing to serve because of the legal and financial risks that membership entails. Even close friends and relatives may turn you down. There is an alternative that is growing in use—an "advisory council."

Assuming you are unable to find individuals with the special experience and knowledge who are willing to serve on your board, you probably have had to resort to using "relatives" in order to meet the requirements of the corporate charter and by-laws. You can still create an outside advisory council to provide you with management assistance. The advisory council has no legal standing or responsibilities derived from or specified in the charter and by-laws. The council is merely an informal group of individuals you have organized to meet with and discuss business as you would do with the board. Taking minutes or holding formal votes on any matter is not necessary.

Under no circumstances should you conduct the council as if it *were* the board. Neither should the council ever meet with the board. Regular board meetings should continue to be held, with minutes taken, to cover all official board matters.

Properly structured and run, the advisory council can provide the benefits of an expert board without the legal exposure of board membership. You should expect to pay a fee to the council members. If you have difficulty finding qualified individuals to serve on your council, contact the business clubs in your area (Rotary Club, Chamber of Commerce, SCORE) for assistance.

You Are Not Alone

Businesses have something else in common with snowflakes besides their fragility: They too are different from one another. Yet, for all their dissimilarity, most businesses share many of the same problems and their owners the same headaches. What this means is that you do not have to reinvent the wheel. If you have a problem, almost certainly someone else has had a similar one in the past and was able to solve it. Even if you think you have no problems, you might have an interest in improving performance or efficiency in one or two areas, and that too has probably been addressed by someone else.

What this means is that you should set some time aside every day to read as much as possible. Try to read a variety of business magazines, books, and newspapers. Any trade magazines or newspapers published for your industry should be required reading for you and your executive staff. Subscribe to several of the business digest publications that extract ideas, suggestions, and comments from a variety of sources covering many topics. Make it common practice to circulate interesting articles among the executive staff.

Chapter 25

Taxes

THE Supreme Court once ruled that the power to tax is the power to destroy. Nowhere is that finding given more credence than by examining the influence that striving for legal tax avoidance or illegal tax evasion has on management when it chooses among the various alternatives. The decision to buy or lease certain assets, plant site selection, financing terms relating to sales, merger and acquisition deals, executive compensation schemes, investments, and many other regular business activities and decisions are frequently twisted and torqued by attempts to manipulate the ultimate tax effect on the deal. While no one can argue that legal minimization of taxes is a desirable objective, it can be argued that too often the costs and effort involved in achieving a low-tax nirvana can sour the entire deal and distort corporate objectives.

Tax Planning

Undeniably, tax planning and consultation before an unusual transaction (acquisition or sale of a business) may result in an entirely new way to structure a transaction to achieve a significant reduction in present or future taxes. It is also possible that creative tax planning may enable you to achieve significant tax reductions on routine business transactions. You should have and use professional tax advisers as part of the resources of the company.

Because tax laws and their interpretation and application change almost daily, tax professionals must spend a significant portion of their time just trying to keep up with the latest changes and interpretations. For this reason, it is probably best that you use an outside professional to provide the tax planning and guidance service for your company.

Don't rely on your own knowledge. If you are providing the right kind of day-to-day leadership to your company, you don't have the time the professionals do to keep up with all the latest tax changes.

Keeping Things in Perspective

Obviously, tax consequences should be given appropriate consideration in the decision-making process. Taxes are a normal cost of doing business—some assessed before you make a profit, others after you've been profitable. Like any cost element, the prudent businessman seeks to hold down tax costs, and so should you. Yet, there is great danger in allowing tax matters to have too high a priority. For one thing, tax laws change, and what seemed like a sweetheart of a deal a few years ago may no longer yield the anticipated results under the latest tax code. Also, your company may be in a totally different situation vis-à-vis taxes with the passage of time.

Almost always there is a price attached to achieving a certain tax status in a business deal. That price, for example, may appear in such form as a higher initial purchase price, a lower cash-flow stream, a sacrifice of flexibility, or additional financial exposure. You can be sure that higher legal and accounting costs will be charged to structure and account for the deal.

When faced with a situation that permits you to choose among tax alternatives, step back for a moment before you allow yourself to automatically pick the tax-saving choice. Review the short-term and long-term implications from a variety of perspectives before you decide. What conditions must remain constant in order for the deal to retain its favorable tax treatment? What flexibility will you have to sacrifice? What difficulties or penalties will you have to contend with if you need more capital in a few years or have to sell or dispose of the property? The old adage "There's no such thing as a free lunch" is quite to the point when applied to tax gimmicks. This doesn't mean some aren't worthwhile, just that you should examine all the possible ramifications first.

Confusion by the Numbers

Because many business managers play games with their company's books, both legally and illegally, the financial statements don't always clearly indicate the company's true status. Frequently, the financial situation has been so distorted by concerns regarding taxes that the information presented in the statements and reports can be misleading at first glance.

When a company's management decides to misstate inventory, all interpretations regarding gross margin, manufacturing costs, even selling prices, can be made meaningless. The same is true when managers skim money from the cash register.

There used to be an old joke about a company keeping two completely different sets of ledgers; a secret, correct one for management and a special set for the tax man. Today, things are more sophisticated: A company may still keep two sets of books, but they're all in one ledger, with a little explanation on the side.

Most certified financial statements have "Notes to the Financial Statements" attached, which give a usually too-brief disclosure of facts relating to some of the items on the balance sheet and P&L statement. One typical note relates to "Income Taxes" and contains information on matters of material tax consequence to the company. Usually there is a reconciliation of the differences between taxes reported on the financial statements and income taxes based on the statutory rate. Many of the reconciling items relate to timing differences (when certain transactions have a tax effect) on such things as depreciation, amortization, reserves, installment sales, and other tax wrinkles.

Since this reconciliation is generally accomplished by grouping such items in major, overall categories, it is practically impossible to recast the effect of the individual reconciling components in order to analyze the detailed operating statements of the company. Not every accounting alternative used in keeping a company's books is an accurate reflection of the true economic and business reality. A company that lets itself get carried away worrying about taxes may actually be impairing its ability to function responsibly and intelligently.

Chapter 26
Going Public

GOING public requires a great deal of advance planning and preparation before you are ready to contact an investment banker. The company's owners and management must do some serious soul-searching regarding the initial public offering (IPO) and the ongoing requirements to which the company will become subject.

Is Everyone Ready?

Managing a company with many shareholders creates an entirely new dimension of fiduciary responsibility for you and the other company officers and directors. Information that once was confidential will have to be disclosed to the public, such as officers' compensation and related party transactions. The public shareholders, the SEC, and representatives (such as research analysts and fund managers) of the financial community will constantly be looking over your shoulder. You may receive external pressure to make decisions in areas you have always considered completely yours (such as payment of dividends or giving short-term profits higher priority). A significant portion of your time and that of many of the company's executives (especially the chief financial officer) will be devoted to investor relations activities, often on an extemporaneous basis. You must also have a competent, articulate chief financial officer who is capable of representing the company in its relationships with its shareholders and the investment community.

Not every company or company management takes the time to investigate how different their working environment will become.

The IPO: Russian Roulette

The decision to take your company public for the first time (and even for subsequent offerings) is similar to deciding to play Russian roulette. It's exciting and downright dangerous. Certainly the rewards are there for the company and its management through a successful IPO—additional equity capital, enhanced company and personal prestige, creation of a market for company stock owned (or under option) by management personnel—but an IPO is still a very big step that many companies and their executives are unprepared for.

To start with, the process may take from six to nine months, even assuming the company is a desirable candidate for a public offering. The definition of a desirable candidate goes beyond the obvious minimum criteria of excellent prospects for future growth, reasonable earnings history, respected management, and company reputation. "Desirability" also includes something that's quite difficult for anyone to predict with confidence—the stock market environment when the actual offering has finally been approved by the Securities and Exchange Commission (SEC) and the market's interest in the stock at that time.

Once a company has decided to "go public," it will probably incur significant legal, accounting, and other expenses on the order of $300,000 or more for the preparation of the "prospectus" and related matters. Having incurred those expenses, the company will have no assurance that the stock offering will take place at all, or that the total amount of funds expected in exchange for public ownership of a designated percentage of stock will be obtained. No one knows for sure whether the public or the financial institutions will be interested in any IPOs (including yours) six or nine months from now, let alone the kind of prices (price/earnings ratios) they would be willing to pay for any given investment opportunity. Thus, a company that was once a "desirable candidate" may no longer be able to generate the anticipated level of investor interest on fickle, volatile, cyclical, sometimes hysterical Wall Street.

The criteria used by those who invest in IPOs are always changing. Some industries become "hot," that is, the market will quickly gobble up almost every offering relating to that "hot" industry until, without warning, it loses interest in that industry. If that happens to your company's offering, your underwriter will have difficulty selling your stock, forcing you to postpone (or withdraw) the offering and/or make a significant reduction in the offering price to make it "more attractive" and easier to sell. Understanding and assessing the risks involved is one of the earliest considerations management must deal with when weighing the possibilities of an IPO of your company's stock.

The Underwriter

The public offering of a company's stock is usually handled by an investment banking firm (alone or in cooperation with others) that, in accordance with the terms of detailed contracts with the company, serves as the middleman in offering the shares to the public. The investment banking firm you select may form a temporary partnership (the "purchasing" syndicate) with one or more other investment banking firms to perform the underwriting function—that is, purchasing a specific number of shares at a specific price from the company (and any selling shareholders at that time). Your investment banking firm may also form a temporary partnership (the "marketing" syndicate) with one or more other investment banking firms to perform the sales function—that is, selling the stock bought by the "purchasing" syndicate to public and institutional investors.

The members of the "purchasing" and "marketing" syndicates are compensated by the difference, or "spread," between the offering price paid by the public or institutional investors and the price the "purchasing" syndicate has agreed to pay the company. A portion of that spread goes to members of each syndicate in accordance with an agreement they have made among themselves.

The spread, usually 7 percent to 12 percent, between the initial offering price to the investor and the price received by the company is influenced by many variables, including the total dollar value of the entire offering: the market conditions existing both at the time of the original discussions with the investment banking firm and later on, at the time of the offering itself; the anticipated and subsequent actual popularity of and interest in the company's stock offering; the size of the participating investment banking firms; the type of underwriting agreement; and how well you negotiate this matter.

The Underwriting Agreement

When you have chosen the investment banking firm to manage your IPO, that firm will have you sign a "letter of intent," which is an outline of the proposed details and terms of the future offering. This letter, signed at the beginning of the IPO process, will probably state that portions of it are only tentative and not binding on either party. In short, the letter allows the investment banking firm to back out of the deal later on, without penalty, for a wide variety of reasons.

Only on or about the day the offering becomes "effective" (receives clearance from the SEC) will the investment banking firm and the company sign the definitive "underwriting agreements." The time between the signing of the "letter of intent" and the "underwriting agreement" may be six to nine months. Under normal circumstances, most reputable investment banking firms will honor the terms as proposed in the earlier letter, but that is not a forgone conclusion. Many things can happen to the company, to the market, to the economic outlook, and to the investment banking company during the interim period. Any one of these could radically alter the terms, if not the prospects, of the offering.

The final, binding underwriting agreement between the company and the investment banking firms is usually one of two types, depending upon the speculative nature of the company's business and future prospects, or its past performance and financial history.

The most desirable arrangement is a "firm commitment underwriting," wherein the underwriter agrees to buy from the company (and from any selling shareholders) all of the stock being offered, at the agreed upon fixed price (offering price minus "spread"). If the underwriter is then unable to find buyers at the offering price for all the stock it has purchased, it must hold any unsold shares for its own account and sell them when it can in the future.

A less desirable arrangement is the "best efforts underwriting," wherein the underwriter agrees only to use its "best efforts" to sell the stock being offered. If unable to sell the stock, the underwriter will not be obligated (as in the "firm commitment" arrangement) to purchase any unsold portion. There are generally two major variations of a "best efforts" underwriting:

1. "All-or-none underwriting," wherein the underwriter agrees to use its "best efforts" to sell the stock, but if it is unable to sell *all* the stock, then *none* is considered sold, and the offering is canceled. The underwriter has no obligation to buy any shares at all.

2. "Minimum percentage underwriting," wherein the underwriter agrees to use its "best efforts" to sell all the stock, but if a certain preset minimum percentage of the total number of shares—say, 50 percent

or perhaps 65 percent—is sold, then the offering is considered accomplished even if the rest aren't sold. The underwriter has no obligation to buy any shares at all.

The type of underwriting arrangement you can expect from the investment banking firm is one of the first things you should discuss with them and include in the "letter of intent." Even though there is no guarantee that conditions will not change later, you must clearly indicate your desire for a "firm commitment" arrangement and try to get it. Talk to several investment banking firms before you agree to any type of underwriting contract other than a "firm commitment." A "best efforts" offering is obviously a much less desirable arrangement, one fraught with additional risks over and above those inherent in any IPO. If, however, it is the only type of arrangement available to you, think long and hard before making the decision to accept or reject it.

Easy Go, Not So Easy Come

Unfortunately, a company spends a considerable amount of "up front" money in connection with a proposed offering. Note the words "proposed offering," for most out-of-pocket expenses and costs will be incurred or committed by the company before and whether or not it ultimately receives one dollar of proceeds from the offering. Expensive lawyers will be reviewing records, contracts, patents, and other papers and agreements you never knew you had. Days will be spent writing, rewriting, and re-rewriting the prospectus and other related materials submitted to the SEC for review. The CPA firm will be reviewing the financial records and statements while it prepares to issue its opinion. A financial printer will begin to set in type the prospectus and other documents, getting ready to print thousands of copies for distribution to potential investors. The investment banking firm may have also insisted upon a "nonaccountable" expense advance at the signing of the letter of intent as part of its compensation package. In addition to these direct out-of-pocket costs, the company will also incur large indirect costs through the diversion of valuable executive time to working on and assisting with the offering. In fact, be careful that you don't allow the day-to-day supervision of the business to suffer through inattention at the same time.

The Brass Ring

A successful IPO is a significant accomplishment in the life of a company and in the careers of its management. For the company, it may permit an opportunity to achieve significant economic growth and success. On a personal basis, it represents an opportunity to acquire considerable wealth, prestige, and power. Certainly there are rewards for the company and its managers in going public. But, as bright as the "brass ring" may appear when you reach out to grab it, make certain you fully understand all the risks.

Afterword

FOR all the millions of businesses in existence throughout the world, it is important to remember that those individuals who have an entrepreneurial spirit and choose to undertake the challenge and burdens of starting or running a business are still a small percentage of the total population. In a world where there are few opportunities to be a pioneer, the business venture remains a unique opportunity for those with the requisite courage and ability. More businesses fail than succeed, yet there are always individuals with drive and determination who are willing to face the financial and emotional risks inherent in starting a business enterprise.

More numerous are the hard-working men and women who become successful business executives. While they may not start or own the business they work for, they still possess the special talents and abilities needed to organize and direct the complex activities inherent in any enterprise. Good judgment, people-management skills, integrity, and the ability to make decisions are common characteristics of the successful business manager.

In our society today, a person engaged in a business activity is frequently vilified. Often unfairly portrayed as being callous, greedy, or dishonest, the average businessperson is none of these. In truth, the typical businessperson is a conscientious, hard-working individual whose efforts, intelligence, and perseverance improve the standard of living of people by providing employment, goods and services. It is an honorable and difficult-to-master profession that does not get the well-earned, positive recognition it deserves.

Bibliography

Belasco, James A., David R. Hampton, and Karl F. Price. *Management Today*, 2d ed. New York: John Wiley & Sons, 1981.

Cohen, Jerome B., and Sidney M. Robbins. *The Financial Manager: Basic Aspects of Financial Administration*. New York: Harper & Row, 1966.

DiPrimio, Anthony. *Quality Assurance in Service Organizations*. Radnor, PA: Chilton Book Company, 1987.

Fallon, William K., ed. *AMA Management Handbook*, 2d ed. New York: AMACOM Special Projects Division, American Management Association, 1983.

Hampton, David R. *Contemporary Management*. New York: McGraw-Hill, 1977.

Herbert, Theodore T. *Dimensions of Organizational Behavior*. New York: Macmillan, 1976.

Hosmer, LaRue T. *Strategic Management*. Englewood Cliffs, NJ: Prentice-Hall, 1982.

Kanter, Rosabeth Moss. *Men and Women of the Corporation*. New York: Basic Books, and Harper Colophon Books, 1977.

Lindsay, Robert, and Arnold W. Sametz. *Financial Management: An Analytical Approach*, 3d ed. Homewood, IL: Richard D. Irwin, Inc., 1963.

McConkey, Dale D. *How to Manage by Results*, 4th ed. New York: AMACOM Book Division, American Management Association, 1984.

Milling, Bryan E. *Cash Flow Problem Solver*, 2d ed. Radnor, PA: Chilton Book Company, 1984.

Mockler, Robert J. *Business Planning and Policy Formulation*. New York: D & R Publishers, 1983.

Niswonger, C. Rollin, and Philip E. Fess. *Accounting Principles*, 12th ed., Cincinatti: South-Western Publishing Company, 1977.

Sherwood, J. F., and Franklin T. Chace. *Principles of Cost Accounting*, 3d ed. Cincinatti: South-Western Publishing Company, 1955.

Tucker, Spencer A. *The Break-Even System: A Tool for Profit Planning.* Englewood Cliffs, NJ: Prentice-Hall, 1963.

Weiss, Martin. *Going Public: How to Make Your Initial Stock Offering Successful.* Blue Ridge Summit, PA: Liberty House, TAB Books, 1988.

Weston, J. Fred, and Eugene F. Brigham. *Managerial Finance*, 3d ed. New York: Holt, Rinehart and Winston, 1969.

White, Richard M., Jr. *The Entrepreneur's Manual.* Radnor, PA: Chilton Book Company, 1977.

Index